Ten Changing Churches

Ten Changing Churches

Editor
Harold Rowdon

Published for

by

paternoster
periodicals

British Library Cataloguing in Publication Data
A catalogue record for this book is available from the British Library

ISBN 0–900128–21–6

Cover design by Paulo Baigent,
typeset by WestKey Ltd., Falmouth,
produced by Jeremy Mudditt Publishing Services, Carlisle,
and published for Partnership by
Paternoster Periodicals, P O Box 300, Carlisle, Cumbria, CA3 9AD.
Printed and bound in Great Britain by Polestar Wheatons Ltd.,
Exeter, Devon.

Partnership

The churches whose story of change is recorded in this volume are a few of the hundred or so which are linked together in the informal fellowship known as 'Partnership'.

They were – and remain – autonomous local churches which proclaim the gospel by word and deed, baptise believers, observe the Lord's Supper, spend time together in worship with or without human leadership, are led by a team of men (and sometimes women), teach the scriptures and pray together.

They sit loose to human traditions, retaining them if they remain valuable but feeling free to amend them if they have become irrelevant or appear unscriptural.

Partnership's role is to provide resources which are beyond the reach of a single local church These include:

- Publications (which include a quarterly magazine, one issue each year being international, with correspondents in about 50 countries; books and booklets; study guides and materials for group Bible study);

- Conferences and consultations (regional, national and international);

- The services of consultants and Bible teachers;

- A matching service, Partnership Link Up Service, which assists churches seeking full-time help.

The cost of subscribing to Partnership is £20 per annum for individuals, and 80p per member for churches (subject to a minimum of £30 and a maximum of £90).

Subscriptions may be sent to the executive chairman, Dr N W Summerton, 52 Hornsey Lane, London N5 6LU (cheques payable to Partnership (UK) Ltd).

Contents

Introduction

It is probably easier to plant a new church than to change an existing one. Churches, like (most) individuals seem to develop an in-built resistance to change, especially when they are convinced that there is only one way for a church to operate to the glory of God – the existing way!

Change is made no easier when there is no well-oiled mechanism for bringing it about; when there has been little or no significant change within living memory; or when there is no widely felt desire for it. Change is unsettling, disturbing, challenging. It upsets the rhythm and routine that most of us find so reassuring. It calls for the breaking of old habits and the forming of new ones. Many people conclude that it is better to stay as we are in the (usually vain) hope that things will improve without all the hassle involved in taking action. And in any case, what action is called for? How can we be sure that it will make any difference: it may make things worse.

* * * * * * * * * * *

Yet this book bears witness to the fact that change is possible and that it can be beneficial. None of the churches described below has any desire to go back to the situation prior to the action that has been taken to bring about change. Stagnation and decline have been replaced by growth which, while rarely dramatic, has been steady and significant. True, one set of problems has been replaced by another; but who in their right mind would want to be delivered from the problems associated with life and growth and return to those of decay and death.

* * * * * * * * * * *

The churches whose recent story is recounted in this volume are not all located in the suburban areas where flourishing evangelical churches are so often to be found. Some are; but others are situated in town centres and rural areas. Nor are they drawn from one particular part of the country, for the west, midlands and north of England are represented, as well as the south-east. They are not entirely confined to England; and there is also diversity in size and culture.

The attentive reader will discern common features in the accounts, which are all written from within by those who have been involved and, usually, have played leading roles in the process of change which they record (though they do not necessarily bear the imprimatur of the leadership or the church as a whole). The editor refrains from specifying the similarities, not wishing to steal the thunder of the authors or to quench the thirst of the reader!

* * * * * * * * * * * *

Each of the churches is involved in Partnership, though this does not necessarily reflect any credit on that network, since Partnership plays no role in the internal affairs of local churches, other than providing stimulus through its publications, its consultations and conferences, its consultants and activists, and through personal interaction. Such stimulus may be received – or ignored – at will.

However, Partnership is concerned to encourage churches to change where this is necessary if their God-given role is to be fulfilled. It is not convinced that 'this is a day of small things'; that we should not expect to see the outpouring of God's Spirit in power since those days are past; nor that faithfulness to tradition is more important than openness to fresh discoveries of God's many-faceted truth. While deeply suspicious of false triumphalism, Partnership believes that a reigning God, an exalted Lord and a dynamic Spirit can change churches today that are despondent, inward-looking, and pessimistic – just as he changed the first disciples on the first Pentecostal day who were in precisely the same situation!

So, please read on.

Harold Rowdon

1

Argyle Chapel, Reading

Ken Speare

Associated with Argyle Chapel since 1961, Ken was for seven years Sunday school superintendent and thereafter an elder for twenty. Latterly, with his wife, he has given himself to pastoral work with some teaching and preaching, Gideon involvement, and the use of evangelistic opportunities.

The church that now meets in Argyle Chapel has an 'Open Brethren' background stretching from the start of the work at Bridge Hall in 1890 to the transfer to Argyle Chapel in October 1959.

LOCATION AND BACKGROUND

The chapel is situated in an older residential neighbourhood which includes blocks of flats, Victorian terraces and modern homes. It has easy access to shops and other facilities on an adjacent main road. Nearby are three schools – a primary school, a private church school and a secondary boys' school. The site of our former church premises on the main road is now part of a busy community centre. We are about fifteen to twenty minutes' walking distance from the centre of Reading, which is part of the so-called silicon-chip valley.

The neighbourhood contains a mixture of younger and older people, including some families with young children, and some residents of Caribbean and Asian origin.

Most of the people within the locality work, though some are unemployed and on benefit. Those who work are mostly employed locally or within Berkshire, but some commute to London which is forty miles away. It is not a particularly affluent area of Reading, but there is a mix of incomes with the result that there are some privately owned homes as well as some rented accommodation.

1

Within the district are an Anglican church and a spiritualist congregation and within easy reach are Baptist, Methodist and independent churches. We have good links with all the evangelical churches.

CONGREGATION

The membership consists of working/middle class people across a wide age range, from young families to senior citizens, drawn from various church backgrounds. We work very happily together, but we would like to see more involvement on the part of all members according to their God-given gifts.

GROWTH

From 1959, individuals and families have joined us as a result of employment moves, and others have left us for the same reason. Growth has been evident in conversions among younger and older people through regular church activities and special evangelistic outreach. On balance, the numbers in fellowship have varied between 100 and 125, and the total congregation on Sunday mornings often exceeds that number. Numerical growth would have been more apparent had we not been involved in church planting, details of which follow in the next section.

RECENT HISTORY

By the early 1960s, Argyle Chapel could be described as a sound 'Brethren' assembly, always outward-looking in evangelism and in Christian fellowship. There was a felt need for a full-time worker. Graham Stokes, who had been involved in SASRA and Open Air Mission, was appointed. The constitution of the church remained unchanged. Graham was in no sense the pastor. He assisted the elders in pastoral work and became the focal point of evangelistic outreach. He was an enabler. He also did some of the teaching and preaching, and represented Argyle Chapel within the town's evangelical community.

The arrangement worked well, although a minority saw it as 'the thin end of the wedge'. After five years Graham moved on to 'Outreach to Industry'. The elders refrained from seeking a replacement. They felt that the church was not ready, and as time went on the idea of a full-time worker seemed to fade. One of the leading elders who had enthusiastically supported Graham could not accept what he saw as the negative outlook of his fellow elders, and left the church.

Early in the 1960s, some of our members who were involved in an outreach on an estate in Tilehurst became a separate congregation, and have since built their own meeting-place. They enjoyed the fellowship and full blessing of the Argyle church. Their numbers now rival those of Argyle Chapel.

In 1968/9 there was a partially successful outreach to drop-outs from society. At about the same time a 'Mother and Toddler' group was introduced. The Sunday school was declining in numbers, but a weeknight outreach to local children was established, and an annual children's holiday Bible club was held. Our Covenanter group had links with similar groups. There were occasional door-knocking outreach efforts, and evangelistic missions were held in 1967, 1970 and 1972. Other activities included the establishment of a branch of the Disabled Christians' Fellowship. Opportunities among senior citizens included occasional lunches, a more spiritually productive coffee morning, and a participatory Bible study session on Saturday mornings.

A monthly Sunday morning family service was introduced in 1975, with communion being celebrated in the evening on such occasions. As this was a departure from normal practice, a few members left the church and declined discussion. One or two others left subsequently over minor issues of practical arrangements, but the general peace of the church was not greatly disturbed.

In the late 1970s, house groups were formed. Elders had for some time been assisted by deacons, in addition to trustees. Women were encouraged to participate in public prayer and worship. This was a gradual process!

Towards the end of the 1970s and into the early 1980s, we were able to assist a local church (with a similar outlook to our own) that had suffered a split. Later we provided them with a pastor and, when he moved on, with another pastor. That church seems to be thriving.

In 1984, we appointed a youth and pastoral worker, John Ayrton, (whose brother, Peter Ayrton, is involved in 'Counties' work). John was with us for three years before going on to 'Interserve'. By this time we all felt the need of a full-time worker, and in January 1988, Harald Holmgren, who had been a missionary in Zambia, and pastor of Ndola Baptist Church, joined us as church pastor and is still with us today. The constitution of the church is unchanged in that Harald is the main teaching and pastoral elder.

In the late 1980s or early 1990s one of our house groups became a focal point for evangelism in a very old district of Reading where they were able to reach people otherwise untouched by Argyle Chapel. Eventually we agreed to accord to them the status of a separate church.

A couple of our members who live in a rural part of Oxfordshire started an outreach among neighbours who now meet regularly in the locality. Another of our members, whose wife teaches in our Sunday school, is also a temporary part-time pastor of North Basingstoke Baptist Church, where there is a growing work.

Ten years ago, we commended a couple to work in Nepal (a doctor and a nurse) with their family. We also support one of our members who works in Zambia, helping churches and church organisations with their financial arrangements. From time to time some of our young people have gone abroad on short-term projects. Several other people who serve overseas have had connections with us and are supported by us.

Locally, we have supported enterprises such as Home Evangelism and FAITH (reaching deprived people). Our pastor, and also some of the members who are Gideons, have opportunities to take assemblies in local schools. With other churches, we are seeking a Reading-based youth worker to extend the work in schools and to support CU groups and the like. In our own neighbourhood door-knocking, a legacy has enabled us to offer scriptures free to all who would welcome God's word. Similarly we have freely loaned copies of the Jesus Video.

Recently we have conducted, and are currently conducting, 'Alpha Courses' both on the church premises and also in one or two homes. We have made a number of good contacts through these activities.

This year we have seen a number of people baptised, including some children. We still have a lot to learn, especially as regards the power of prayer, spiritual commitment and the use of all the spiritual gifts God has given us. To God be the glory! Without him we can do nothing.

STRENGTHS AND TRADITIONS

Bible teaching has always been a strong tradition among 'Brethren'. So has weekly breaking of bread/communion'. Apart from monthly family or guest services on Sunday mornings, when we break bread in the evening, our normal practice is to have both systematic Bible exposition and communion in the morning, and further teaching and prayer in the evening. The needs of unsaved people are not overlooked. Sadly, Sunday evening attendances do not match those of the morning.

Missionary weekends, a 'Spiritual Renewal' weekend, Tearfund Sunday, and special seasonal outreach, have provided opportunities for stimulating and challenging both believers and nonbelievers. A church 'awayday' (or a weekend) for special studies has been fruitful, as has also the reporting back by pastor/elders who have attended special conferences. 'Support groups' have recently taken over the work of deacons, involving more people, with each group concentrating on a particular activity, ranging from administration to evangelism, from pastoral care to disseminating prayer needs. Elders are also involved, but they try to give themselves increasingly to prayer and Bible study, to a God-given vision for the church, and to overall pastoral care.

CHANGES/OBSTACLES

Changes have been gradual. A few defections have already been mentioned but, on the whole, harmony has been maintained. When encouraging sisters' participation, we took time not only publicly to open up the scriptures but also to visit people in their homes for discussion. When it was felt necessary to ensure that the whole church was behind the intended appointment of our present pastor, we held a special church meeting to air the proposal, and then arranged for Harald to come home from Zambia in order to spend time in Reading visiting elders and leaders in their homes for fellowship, prayer and discussion, and to preach at Argyle. Of course, there have been differences of opinion over minor matters, but by the grace of God unity has been maintained.

WEAKNESSES

It has been difficult to get long-term commitment for youth work, which itself diminished with the abolition of Covenanter groups. Door-knocking outreach and open-air evangelism are sometimes attempted, but remain unpopular. Some pubs have been visited with song and guitar, but this is not an easy task. There remains a vast field of need all around us.

Moving from maintenance to mission is an uphill road! Alpha is presenting new opportunities. Former 'Discovery' and 'Just Looking' groups will probably open up again along with 'Nurture' groups, as new contacts are made. We have many dedicated workers, including gifted and energetic ladies, one of whom, a social worker, is opening up opportunities among Christians for Care Remand Fostering. But we are only touching the fringe of need.

PROSPECTS

Through commitment, prayer and the use of everyone's gifts, we need to go forward in fulfilment of the task God has entrusted to us. In all this, we must remember God's eternal purpose to make us more like Jesus (Gal 5:22–23). Activity must never be a substitute for spirituality. 'For from Him and through Him and to Him are all things. To Him be the glory for ever! Amen.'

2

Christ Church, Woodbury, Devon

The cost of change

Henry Fulls

Henry is married to Jennifer, and they have three sons and six grandsons. He is managing director of a shoe distribution company, working with his sons; became a church elder when still in his twenties; and is currently studying part-time with Trinity Theological College in Bristol. An avid reader, he has recently discovered the Internet. His ambition is to be able to take all his grandchildren to Disneyworld.

Woodbury is a large village with a population of around 3,000, situated in East Devon, between Exmouth and Exeter. The entirely Anglo-Saxon population contains a high proportion of elderly people, some of whom have retired to the area. A number of families have lived in the village for generations, and a few still work on the land. Increasingly, professional people move into the area, commute into Exeter during the week, and enjoy country life at weekends.

The village has retained several shops, two pubs, a thriving village hall, and an historic parish church, St. Swithun's, though recently this has lost its vicar and now shares one with an adjoining parish. Several caravan sites on the village outskirts bring an influx of visitors during the summer months. Perhaps Woodbury's main claim to fame is as the home of the recently built Nigel Mansel Golf Club.

There are a number of small villages to the north of Woodbury which have only a parish church (usually without full-time clergy) or no church at all. To find another 'free' church it is necessary to travel to Exmouth (5 miles) or Exeter (8 miles).

MOVING HOUSE

In 1882 two 'Brethren' evangelists conducted a tent campaign in Woodbury. As a result of this, twelve people – five men and seven women – left one or other of the two existing churches to form an assembly. At first they met in each other's homes, then in a builder's shed. As the assembly grew (to forty members by 1897) the need for premises increased and a Napoleonic drill-hall was rented and later purchased. Numbers, though, did not move much above forty, but the Lord blessed the work quietly whilst other events unfolded.

The building and name of Christ Church originated out of the mid-nineteenth-century Oxford Movement, which attempted to lead the Church of England into a more 'high church' style of worship. When, in 1847, the vicar began to introduce such changes into St. Swithun's the more evangelical of his congregation were so incensed that they departed to build their own church, a plain, red-brick nonconformist chapel. Built in 1851, it affiliated to the Free Church of England under the name of Christ Church.

Between the wars, the Free Church of England cause in the village folded. The building was taken over, first by the Methodists and then by the Baptists, but both failed to maintain a live church and, by 1967, Christ Church was deserted and in a poor state of repair. However, the drill-hall, known by then as Broadway Chapel, was in an even worse state, with rampant wood-worm, dry rot and a very seriously leaking roof. After much prayer and consideration, the 'Brethren' decided to acquire and renovate Christ Church. This was a major step for an assembly of only forty-five members, but after a further two years of hard work and financial sacrifice the move was finally made in 1969.

During this period most of the children in the village would have attended the Sunday school, with many going on to the youth fellowship and Bible class. Visionary men had already begun a weekly youth club, with games and activities followed by an 'epilogue'. There were few teenagers in Woodbury for whom this was not a regular and keenly anticipated part of the week.

GOING FORWARD

The change to a new building provided an opportunity to make changes to the structure of the services, with a view to making the church more acceptable to people outside the 'Brethren' tradition. The morning 'breaking of bread' was prefaced by ministry from a prearranged speaker and the time given to open worship was reduced. These changes proved popular, and the congregation grew, reaching eighty by 1988. This growth was achieved in part by the increasing size of Woodbury, which brought Christians into the village often from other denominations, but also through a whole variety of outreaches.

In 1989 the church used a course called *Person to Person* which encouraged personal evangelism. Those who did the course – a great majority of the church – were encouraged to embark upon some form of local outreach. For several, this took the form of distributing a questionnaire which was sent to many of the local residents asking, among other things, whether they would be interested in attending an informal study group investigating the claims of the Bible. At much the same time two other members began *Agnostics Anonymous*, which involved inviting non-Christian friends to their homes where, over 'beer and crisps', they chatted about life, the universe – and Jesus Christ. Most importantly, the whole church was behind these outreaches and several older folk contracted to pray daily and at length for God's blessing on the enterprises.

The results were impressive. One person after another professed conversion and, for a time, there was a real feeling of revival in the air. About fifteen people with very little church background were added to the congregation in a very short time and it seemed that the whole village became aware that God was at work in Woodbury.

We were also a sending church. Over a long period the church had been able to give financial support to several young people preparing for further ministry by attending Bible college.

Alongside the directly evangelistic outreach, another humanitarian venture was being realized. Through the vision of one member, the church became involved in transporting food and other aid to Romania, and *Christ Church Aid for Romania* was born. Recently changed to *Christian Response to Eastern Europe*, this work has been mightily blessed with in excess of £2,000,000 of aid sent out to date. The local inhabitants who contributed, and encouraged others to contribute, showed great interest. Each convoy was sent off after a short time of public prayer and praise, often conducted in the village centre. The name of Christ Church, Woodbury, became widely known and respected in the area. Within two years the congregation had grown to over 140, with half living in the village and half coming from the surrounding towns and villages. Special discipling house groups were set up for the new Christians and it seemed that we really were 'praising God and enjoying the favour of all the people' (Acts 2:47).

MIXED CONGREGATION

This outreach had resulted in a changing congregational mix. Three distinct groupings were emerging: the original congregation, mostly conservative and with strong 'Brethren' connections; those coming from other churches, several with a charismatic background; and the new converts with very little Christian background at all, but keen and open to new ideas.

The revival, if such it may be called, slowly faded away, and we began to realise that we were facing the problems that change brings.

TIME FOR CHANGE

When the church was comfortably full, or nearly so, it seemed right to make plans to extend our site. There were many indications that the time was right for us to apply for planning permission to relocate to a green field site near to the centre of the village, close to the school and the elderly residential dwellings. The church was keen, and an option was obtained on the piece of land in question, with just enough in the building fund to cover its full cost. Ambitious plans were drawn up for a modular construction and seating for 300 plus, together with an adjoining sports hall. The cost was estimated to be around £500,000. As it turned out, we were in for a bumpy ride. For in the event something else was happening.

Slowly, but very surely, cracks were beginning to appear. Two of our greatest 'prayer warriors' died. Several of those running the outreach work began to feel that they lacked the wholehearted support of the church. There was emerging a differing of emphases on certain doctrinal matters and a feeling by some that the forms of service should be amended. There was pain, there was hurt, there was conflict and misunderstanding; with resulting unrest and uncertainty within the fellowship. Some left us, of whom some returned to the churches whence they had come, others sought new ones, while some, sadly, seemed to go nowhere. Most, though, remained, albeit in a state of confusion and carrying the marks of their wounding. The plans for our new church building began to attract hostility from a small but vociferous minority within the village. This culminated in a full-scale public meeting, with the added interest of the local press. Indeed we were experiencing 'fightings within and fears without'. The vision had gone. Why? All had been going so well, God had blessed the work of his people, souls had been added to the kingdom. Why had things gone wrong? Some hurt is still apparent, but the story needs to be told if only so that others – the many others – who have been this way, or may still traverse this path, can be encouraged and helped to know that, through such change, God brings new life, new vision and a new sense of community among his people.

A CRISIS OF IDENTITY

How were we to handle this confusion – this *crisis of identity*? There were several obvious scenarios.

The immediate reaction was to pursue a middle of the road approach and, especially in worship, to seek to contain the extremes of both styles in one service. But this was gradually seen to be self-defeating. Most people could find something in the service, but no-one was totally satisfied.

So what other options should we consider?

One option would be to change over completely to the new way of worship and church life. The new vibrancy, warmth of relationships, supremacy of prayer, sharing each other's burdens, the openness and challenge, would be our way forward. The fresh awareness of the nearness of Christ and the sense of the power of the Spirit, together with the importance of praise and worship, would lift the church to new heights of spirituality. Our experience of what we had for long believed would now become real, and our giftings would be realised as never before. The church would be challenged again, feelings of failure and defeat would be exchanged for renewal and evangelism.

What made us think again was the realisation that, to many, the externals of such worship were foreign since they had been used to a quieter, more reflective, traditional form of worship. The emotional involvement that would be needed would be an embarrassment to many. (Yet many of these features were what we had been waiting many years for, including the breaking down of barriers and the introduction of things that would touch the heart and penetrate beneath the veneer so often apparent in our services.)

Another option was to outlaw all attempts to alter in any way the status quo, expressed in the following ways. The new choruses lack much theological content, the tunes are banal, dirgeful or just triumphalist. And why, oh why, repeat them so many times? The hymns of Wesley and Watts are full of biblical teaching. It is through the reading and the teaching of the word that Christ speaks to people today and touches their hearts. House groups are good but it is in the church building that folk gather to hear the word. The music group is alright (in its place) but it is noisy. Why change? God has blessed us mightily in the past.

A third option was to have two quite separate 'churches'. The more traditional congregation would continue to meet in the normal way while the others would meet at a separate time, perhaps not even on a Sunday. Everyone would be welcomed to both types of service. Outreach could then be pursued more enthusiastically by each group without the 'cringe' element that would be experienced in meeting together. Each group would help to facilitate the development of both congregations.

A fourth option was to plant a new church. Our difficulties could provide an opportunity for some to move into the neighbouring village just a mile or so away and begin a new work.

Throughout this time many folk were coming under increasing pressure from their peers. Many, not fully understanding the issues involved, simply saw differences of opinion gradually becoming more acute and love being pushed to the sidelines. We had to face the fact that some were going to leave. We so much wanted that warm relationship that ought to characterise Christians, but felt it slowly ebbing away. Paul's problem in Corinth seemed to be working itself out within our own church. There was a variety of personalities, and some identified with 'Apollos', others with 'Cephas' and some with 'Paul'. Our quest became: 'How can we find a way to worship and work together while recognising the value of each member of our church?'

It was felt to be of vital importance that the leadership should be united, and seen to be united, in every aspect of the situation. Although embracing differing views on several issues of both principle and practice, it was felt appropriate to produce a document that laid out what we felt was right for the church at that particular moment. This would be a document which all the leadership could subscribe to and seek to implement.

In the event, we failed. The paper proved to be a catalyst among the leadership and the inevitable happened. The differences among us became irreparable, and one elder resigned.

Gradually a fifth option began to be seen as perhaps a viable alternative. Why not continue as we were but take on board the best of the new worship and the best of the elements of the more traditional congregation. Let us give time to the development of the new ways and encourage all members of the congregation to be encouragers of each other. But could it be done – had it worked before? Those who felt that this was something that might succeed put their efforts into the cause.

The discerning reader may have noticed that this fifth option is not greatly different from the 'middle of the road' option rejected earlier, before all the options were considered. In fact it *is* different – the difference is chronological. Things that can be achieved after a lengthy period of time are different from the limited range of choices that seem fitting in the midst of pressure. When, once again, we can begin to prefer each other's needs to our own and when each can gradually affirm the other, healing comes. When there is encouragement instead of criticism, when there is a going out to the other instead of a withdrawing from them, and when love replaces fear, then any option is possible; but especially this one which will bind the church together rather than draw it apart.

A NEW LEADERSHIP STRUCTURE EVOLVED

The existing eldership was becoming aware of several folk within the fellowship who were exhibiting leadership qualities and who would benefit from being recognised as leaders. It was apparent that the church itself was looking for this. These men, and one woman, joined the existing elders as a leadership team. Their particular theological outlooks, though varying widely, were not counted as important in the light of the belief that God was calling them to accept this role within the church. It seemed, again, to be the desire of the church, and of the new leadership team, that there should still be a small group of elders.

The function of the leadership team is to take all major decisions of the church. The function of the eldership is to be especially responsible for the sensitive personal issues, to seek a vision for the church, to have time away from the business generally in order to pray. We have been blessed with godly men who have been able to recognise when it was time to lay aside the responsibilities of eldership. We have one part-time paid administrator, and one of the elders, who has a pastor's heart, has contracted to give to the church part of each week.

The age range of our small eldership team is 34 to 63. There is still some difference of theological and practical interpretation in this eldership. We now view this as a healthy tension that need not be stressful, with each one carrying a burden for a particular aspect of church life. One feels for the traditional part of the church – another for the charismatic. This tension is undergirded by the felt need for unity and love and respect for other members of the team.

Historically, it may have been the case that the elders of 'Brethren' churches have to a considerable extent been of one mind over most (all?) matters. But this has been a unity sometimes formed under pressure to conform to what others may expect or demand. As a result, minority rule can carry the day and change becomes an impossibility.

A NEW 'MANY-PERSON' MINISTRY EVOLVED

The main functions of the church are cared for by teams, each with a leader who is responsible to the leadership team. (It sounds messy and fuzzy, but for the present it works!)

These ministry teams are responsible for:

• Evangelism and mission

Sending It has always been important for us to be a sending church. So it has been a real encouragement for the church to find that several of its members were being called to Christian service. At least two families have been supported through Bible college. One family has spent four years in Nepal with INF, and part of our commitment to them was to send out someone personally to visit them while they were away. Currently we contribute to someone's full-time course at college, and are about to help support another couple when they take up a pastorate in a small church. One person is serving full-time with YWAM in Albania and depends on us for most of her support.

The elderly Thursday Trippers was the vision of two men who have a heart for the older folks. Each month, a trip is arranged into the surrounding area with tea on return. Any in the village may come, and in fact most who come are non-churched folk.

The middle-aged Friends and Neighbours is another bridge to the village. Each month there is a presentation of a matter of interest, followed by a brief epilogue and coffee. The format pre-dates Alpha but draws a lot of people to hear the gospel. The weekly coffee morning is another place to meet, chat and relate to members of the church.

The team is responsible to focus on conversions. A new initiative to bring friends into the church and to introduce them to Christ is being planned for the autumn/winter.

• Prayer and house groups

These have been introduced in order to encourage the church in the ministry of prayer and relationship building. Housegroups became the 'buzz' word among the churches a decade or so ago. It is our experience that they appeal to some but not to others. Many who participate find them a real benefit to their spiritual growth.

• Youth and children's work

Beside the regular Sunday clubs, one of the major village events of the year is Holiday Club. Parents now arrange their holidays around this date. This event has been mostly run by the team. One person is recognised as the leader and his job in the church is to organise and run the club, with its follow-up Friday night 'bash'. Originality has known few bounds. Activities may be based on ideas culled from current TV prime spots, and the last club showed a vague similarity in some of its content to a certain house party and was complete with the 'gunge tank'. A float in the local carnival was well accepted by the parents and an entry in the well-publicised Exeter Carnival became a tool for sharing the gospel through song, visuals and leaflet distribution.

The menace being caused by local, and not so local, teenagers became such a concern that a public meeting was called to prepare a plan of campaign. So Christ Church re-started a long-established youth club after two members felt a call upon their lives to be involved in such a work. Their committee comprises some of the parents of the teenagers from outside the church and, although the potential for difficulty is there, the opportunity for good is greater. It does require strong leadership, but every effort is being made to communicate the love of God to these folk who seem to have very little knowledge of Christian things. Another evening has been designated as a drop-in time for any of the young people to have coffee and come to terms with the real issues.

• Maintenance

Plans are now in hand to develop the existing site.

• Social events

The team feels a need to develop the 'togetherness' of the church by fostering relationships. Events are arranged, such as walks, barbecues, visits to the panto, quiz nights, a barn dance, and the bi-annual weekend away at a hotel in North Devon. Almost all of these events draw in some from outside the church to join us, and provide yet another bridge-building opportunity.

• Pastoral care

The team comprises folk with a genuine desire that no one is overlooked, and the gift of knowing when someone needs encouragement. A regular visitation programme of people who are elderly or infirm is included.

A NEW FORMAT FOR OUR SERVICES EVOLVED – AND WILL CONTINUE TO EVOLVE

Our main service of the week is on Sunday mornings. This is the time for our teaching and our communion, but included in the service is a time for the children that really *is* for them. We want God to be at work among us. We seek to involve as many of the congregation as possible. One will lead our prayers, another do the Bible reading, another talk to the children, another chair and lead communion. Sometimes the music group participates; sometimes it's organ and piano. Except for family services, our morning always concludes with communion, following on from the teaching of the scripture.

We now use Sunday evenings as an opportunity to have a variety of services. Some are the responsibility of a team of (mainly) younger folk and are of a more contemporary style, majoring on testimony, prayer and worship led by the music group. On other Sundays a more traditional service caters for the needs of the slightly older (usually) members of the church. Often, Sunday evening is the time when visitors come to the church, and the emphasis is increasingly on services that appeal as much as possible to all age groups.

CONCLUSION

The undercurrents of criticism have diminished as those who found it difficult to live with the situation have moved away, while our search for an identity has helped us re-focus on the things that really matter.

We have a greater appreciation of the things that before we feared or were suspicious of. And through it all we have had the opportunity to re-think what the important matters really are, and to learn from one another.

But nagging questions remain. Can the old culture and the new meet together? Can baby boomers, generation X'ers and senior citizens joy in the Lord and learn of him together? Can the gaps be bridged – the generation gap, the cultural gap, the expectation gap, the theological gap? Do churches have to go to their graves suffering a terminal illness for years before they die? Will those who desire a relational, tactile, more extroverted style of worship and experience be able to adapt to the needs of reflective, private folk,who have been schooled in their ways of worship over many years? Will the traditionalists be able to accept the ways of the new worship and lifestyle? Can we live together, work together and worship together?

Sometimes we wonder – but we are beginning to believe we really can! It deserves our all to try, for there is a world out there that depends on it.

3

Greenford Gospel Church, Middlesex

Jon Watts

*Jon grew up among the 'Gospel Standard' group of 'Strict
Baptists'. He was converted at agricultural college and served as
student chairman of the UCCF colleges department. After studying
at London Bible College he has been at Greenford Gospel Chapel
since 1982 (pastor since 1989).*

Greenford is an unlikely location for church growth. Sandwiched
in north-west London between the densely populated areas of
Wembley and Southall on the one hand, and the more affluent
Harrow and Ealing on the other, Greenford is a mass of 1930s
'London overspill' terrace housing mixed with industry. During the
last twenty years, there have been great social demographic changes
in the area, as the original generation of home owners died and the
properties were bought as first homes. Greenford has increasingly
become a utility area, with people moving in for a short time for
cheaper housing and proximity to work. The racial and religious
profile has also changed dramatically with a high proportion of
housing now being purchased by Sikhs, Hindus and Muslims.

Sadly, the local church situation is pretty grim. With the exception of a growing, charismatic, Anglo-Catholic church, and a
healthy Baptist church, the other local churches, whether Anglican,
Baptist, 'Brethren' or Free Church, are in decline or even terminally
ill. The normally virile Kensington Temple satellite congregations
have not found Greenford and Northolt easy areas in which to plant
and grow.

Why then has Greenford Gospel Church doubled in size during
the nineties? Why has the church had to extend its premises? Why is
the church expected to grow even more in the future? The answers

to these questions may become clear as the story of the development of the church is recounted.

ROOTS

The church's roots go back to the 1860s, when a cottage mission was started in the tiny hamlet of Greenford Green by Sir William Perkin, founder of the analine dye factory in Oldfield Lane. This village mission was supported by evangelists who travelled out to 'poor dark Greenford' from Ealing.

In the early 1920s, responsibility for the mission was taken over by the 'Brethren' at Grove Hall, Ealing, and Greenford Gospel Hall was officially founded. Towards the end of the 1920s, a small piece of land was purchased on the other side of Oldfield Lane adjacent to the Grand Union Canal and, in the early '30s, the members of the independent Greenford Gospel Hall built their own hall, constructed mostly of wood. With the massive development of Greenford in the mid 1930s, the assembly grew and developed, with particular emphasis on evangelism and children's work. In 1958, the wooden building was replaced with a new, modern hall with four small rooms for children's work and smaller meetings. Throughout the next decade, the church had an unusually strong youth work with evangelistic coffee bars etc. The young people were represented on the eldership by younger men who had considerable vision.

FIRST FULL-TIME WORKER

One result was the appointment, in 1969, of Peter Morris, a young LBC graduate, as a full-time worker. Within a short time of Peter's appointment, the church suffered one of many 'brain drains' with a number of the visionaries moving out of the London area for better housing and career choices. Peter enthusiastically threw himself into developing the evangelistic and youth emphasis of the assembly. Much good work was done, but progress and growth was limited by the hostility of the elders to the charismatic movement which was influencing many of the young people at that time. Some disheartened and discouraged young people drifted away, and the church settled down in the 1970s and early '80s to remaining a highly active, evangelistic, 'Brethren' assembly of around 80–100 members, consisting mostly of converts of the church and those of long standing 'Brethren' background.

In 1982 Peter Morris, now the driving force of the church, launched 'Good News Down The Street', an Anglican initiative for evangelism widely used by churches of all traditions. GNDS was extremely effective in mobilising the church and, as a result, between twenty and thirty people were converted in the space of two years. Many of the converts were younger people of Afro-Caribbean background who immediately began to challenge the principles and practices of a 'Brethren' assembly. A monthly family service had already been introduced, but the protected Sunday morning breaking of bread meeting and the traditional evening gospel service were now being ravaged by a group of enthusiastic new Christians who had no 'Brethren' background and little interest in becoming 'Brethren'. However, these new converts certainly had an enthusiasm for the Lord and a zeal to reach their friends with the gospel.

Peter urged the church towards the radical changes needed to accommodate these new Christians. The rest of the eldership, while welcoming the growth, resisted substantial change. The result was that many of the new Christians became frustrated, and thirteen of the Afro-Caribbean young people left to form their own charismatic fellowship. The influx of new Christians had raised issues that would not go away and, over the next few years, changes took place that included a greater openness to the work of the Spirit, the change of name to Greenford Gospel 'Church' rather than 'Hall', permission for women to participate in the breaking of bread meeting, and the lifting of the restriction on speaking in tongues.

ANOTHER FULL-TIME WORKER

In 1985 the church appointed another young LBC graduate, Jon Watts, and his wife, Tricia, as assistant and youth co-ordinator. Four years later, after more than twenty years of ministry at Greenford, Peter and Phyllis Morris moved on. It was a time of great change for the church. Within five years, around sixty members had moved out of London or had died. The church asked Jon to take over Peter's role and become pastor. Jon had made it clear to the church that, if they wanted him to stay, he required a mandate for change – which included the complete restructuring of the programme of Sunday services.

Jon also presented a four-fold vision of church growth for the '90s, based on Acts 2: 42-47: Growing up/ Growing together/ Growing Out/ Growing Bigger. The aim was to build on Greenford's strong history of evangelism and to create a 'user-friendly' church. In 1990, the services were changed to an 11.00 am morning worship with groups for 0–11 year-olds (later extended to 0–17 years) with an alternating evening worship/communion and a 10.00 am early communion on two Sundays a month. Morning worship saw immediate growth, with parents attending from the first week. By 1991, numbers at morning worship had increased to 100 (including children).

PRAYER AND FASTING

There was a growing awareness in the church of the importance of prayer and fasting and, in September 1991, the church was called to a week of prayer before the autumn activities commenced. The impact of this week was so encouraging that it was repeated at the beginning of 1992. Largely through the initiative of Andy Radford (later to train at Moorlands College and become our part-time evangelist and schools worker), the weeks of prayer were extended to months of prayer and fasting, in March and again in June of 1992. Significant conversions and developments took place in each of these months.

RAPID GROWTH

By the time of the month of prayer in September 1992, the congregation had grown to 110. September 13 saw 130 people in church and September 20, 150 people, with many unable to sit down until children had left the church. That week 160 new chairs were bought and the church was reorganised to accommodate more people. Harvest Sunday, 27 September, saw over 200 pile into the building. Since that time, the average congregation has never dropped below 170 people, despite the fact that during that period well over 50 members moved away from the area.

In addition to prayer and fasting, other factors contributed to that September growth. In August, our annual children's holiday club had proved to be particularly popular and successful, encouraging parents to bring their children to church. We had also run a very fruitful Greenford Frontier Camp for 10–15 year-olds (the camps had been started in 1990). The bulk of the growth at this time was of 'fringe' attenders (mostly parents bringing their children). However, during 1992, the church also benefited by some transfer growth from other churches.

LEADERSHIP TEAMS

The sudden growth of the church in 1992 created impossible burdens for the eldership and necessitated the speedy introduction of leadership teams to press forward the work of the church. In addition to the existing business committee and evangelism committee, there were added a worship team, pastoral team, children's and youth team.

The introduction of the worship team and the pastoral prayer team had an immediate impact on the style of the services and resulted in considerable opposition by some of those of 'Brethren' background, who, by now, were a minority but still held much power in the church.

COMMUNITY PROFILE

During the 1980s and '90s, the church benefited from an increasingly higher profile in the community. In the 1970s, Peter Morris had started building up links with local schools by taking occasional assemblies and RE lessons. In the '80s and '90s, this was expanded to all the primary schools and some high schools, with the use of professional communicators such as the Saltmine Theatre Company, sketch-board artists and Christian magicians. With Andy Radford's appointment in 1994 as our part-time evangelist and schools worker, the work in schools has continued to expand across the borough of Ealing to several thousand children every term, including a regular Christian lunchtime club in one of the high schools. The involvement in schools has led to other opportunities. Schools have approached the church to request us to become school governors, and we are also represented on the Ealing Borough SACRE (Standing Advisory Committee on Religious Education). The results have been that, through Andy, our schools worker, there are very few children and young people in the community who do not know the name of Greenford Gospel Church. The reputation and credibility of the church has also been enhanced by the many positive comments and recommendations of teaching professionals.

In 1992, the church was at the forefront of a public inquiry into the proposed closure of a local road by the industrial giant, Glaxo, whose world headquarters are situated opposite the church. The road closure clearly disadvantaged the church and the local community, and the church spearheaded the campaign against the closure which resulted in a public enquiry lasting several weeks. The largely non-professional local community were almost unanimous in their support and appreciation of our willingness to stand up for them. The campaign also earned us respect from our MP, MEP, councillors, press, and representatives of industry. Part of the enquiry took place in the church building, and the pastor was invited to address several public meetings. Although the road was subsequently closed, the church benefited from a greatly enhanced reputation in the community, and a grant of £23,600 towards a new building!

The impact of the church's leadership in the road closure campaign has led to MPs, councillors, and local industry seeking our opinion and advice regarding local issues such as road improvements and community benefits. It has also led to the church's high profile in the ongoing campaign for the building of a new high school in the community.

RACIAL DIVERSITY

Since 'Good News Down The Street' in the 1980s, the racial mix of the church has gradually developed to the point where the church has around twenty different nationalities represented, including a number converted from Muslim and Sikh backgrounds. In this way the church has become more reflective of the local community with all its rich diversity.

Its diversity of racial background has given the church many opportunities for cross-cultural mission. It has led the church into supporting an Asian evangelist, and the production of the *Asian Focus* magazine. A young family have gone out to Afghanistan, and another girl is training for youth evangelism in Europe. The church is informally twinned with a similar church in Brazil, and children raise money for children's work in Brazil. The congregation has many natural family links with countries around the globe (some of which experience active persecution against Christians). All this enables the church to have a prayerful influence far beyond the boundaries of Greenford.

BUILDINGS

The church building was extended in 1983, with the addition of a rear hall, kitchen, small office and toilets. In 1994, a house adjacent to the church was purchased for the pastor and by 1995 two rooms in the house were being used on Sunday mornings for the expanding children's and youth work. In 1997, after several years' delay, major rebuilding and extension work on the church was commenced at the cost of £175,000. The end result has been the appearance of a brand new church in Greenford.

ALPHA

In September 1995, the evangelism committee urged the church to use Alpha courses as the main evangelistic thrust. Again, this met with some opposition owing to its charismatic emphasis, and resulted in the loss of an elder. The decision was made to go for Alpha instead of the existing house groups (some of which were a cause for concern). Alpha was an immediate success, leading to the conversion of well over thirty people, as well as the rededication and spiritual renewal of many more. Such was the success of the first Alpha course that every person who had taken it was keen to go on to the Beta course, created to integrate existing church members and Alpha converts into an ongoing nurture and study programme.

The success of Alpha and Beta created some major issues in the church. Once again, the church had a major influx of new, enthusiastic, Spirit-filled Christians who had little interest or sympathy for traditional 'Brethren' background, practice or theology. Running two mid-week courses as well as Sunday services and all the ongoing children's and youth work also highlighted the desperate shortage of gifted spiritual men in the church able to give good teaching. As a result, the elders decided to allow women to give the occasional Alpha and Beta talk.

Sadly, a few with traditional backgrounds reacted against Alpha and Beta, and the use of women to teach. This led to two years of attrition and disunity which, in the end, resulted in the drawing up of a new trust deed, and the resignation of all the elders. Thankfully, during this time the majority of the church were unaware of the power struggles that were taking place, and the Lord in his mercy was adding monthly to the church with eighteen baptisms in fifteen months (sixteen being a direct result of Alpha and Beta).

NEW VISION AND NEW DIRECTION

In the summer of 1997, in the middle of all the building developments, Jon Watts urged the church towards a new vision and a new direction in which to go when the new building was finished. In November 1997, sixteen days before the opening of the new building, the elders stepped down. On 29 March 1998, a new leadership team, comprising men and women, was commissioned to take the church in a new direction with a new vision in a new building.

A handful of people whose 'Brethren' background made them feel unable to be part of these changes have moved on. However, within the first few months of this new beginning, others have asked for baptism and church membership. The expectation in the church is that the Sunday morning congregation will outgrow the new building, and that consideration will have to be given to an alternative venue, or church planting.

WHAT ARE FELT TO BE THE KEY FACTORS IN GROWTH AT GREENFORD GOSPEL CHURCH?

Leadership by full-time workers

Greenford as a church in a 'blue collar' area has not been blessed with many gifted and able elders or lay leaders. Because of this, it has been unusually dependent on the leadership and gifting of its full-time workers. It is hard to imagine that Greenford would have been any different from the other local 'Brethren' assemblies which are generally small, elderly and declining, had it not been for the leadership and vision of its full-time workers.

Particular mention must be made of Peter and Phyllis Morris, whose long-term commitment and zeal prepared the church for growth and development. Continuity and stability of full-time leadership has enabled the church to build on the changes and development of the past. Since 1969, the church has never been without a full-time worker, two in all. Moreover, as Jon Watts worked with Peter Morris for four years before taking over as pastor, he has been able to build on the past, making radical changes and yet providing continuity.

Vision

Leadership and vision are almost inseparable. Since 1989 the church has been presented with a clear vision for the future. This has helped to give purpose and direction for activities within the church. Substantial growth has taken place in all activities from Sunday club to senior citizen groups. The collective result of this growth has resulted in the Lord blessing the vision of the church more abundantly than we could have dreamed or imagined.

Prayer and Fasting

We believe that prayer and fasting has been the most important key to growth. Weeks, months and 40 days of prayer and fasting continue to be an integral part of the church programme. This has led to a hunger for a deeper knowledge and experience of God, a passion for the lost, and a hunger for renewal and revival. This emphasis on prayer and fasting has been criticized and rejected by a minority who felt it was encouraging too much spiritual intensity.

Evangelism

Greenford has a long history of evangelistic motivation. The desire of the church as a whole to reach out with the gospel of Jesus Christ has led to numerous activities including open-air meetings, special missions, coffee bars, evangelistic meals, fun days, leafleting, door-to-door work, holiday clubs, camps, parents and toddlers groups, etc. In recent years we have sought to build on this strength with 'Good News Down the Street', Alpha and other initiatives.

Change

Evangelistic growth has been inseparably linked with changes in the church. The greatest changes have taken place during times of an influx of new Christians. In order to accommodate their needs it has been necessary to adapt and change older styles and practices. The evangelistic motivation of the majority of the church has often made painful changes more palatable. Change has not been for change's sake, but for the sake of reaching and keeping newer Christians. The church sees itself as a mission station reaching out to the community. To some extent, the needs of church members are considered secondary to reaching out with the gospel to non-members. The priority that the church has given to evangelism has been a vital key to its growth.

The Holy Spirit

It is easy to give intellectual assent to the fact that no real church growth can take place without the activity of the Holy Spirit. However, it is also easy for a church to neglect the dynamic of the Spirit in its structured programmes, meetings and even evangelism.

In recent years at Greenford there has been an increasing desire to be more open to, and dependent upon God's Holy Spirit. This has led to a greater faith and an increased hunger to hear from God and to be led as a church by him. Gradually, we have been able to teach people to expect to experience the biblical reality of God, as well as to give intellectual assent to a biblical theology of salvation. This paradigm shift has resulted in significant changes in our teaching, worship and evangelism. We find ourselves in the situation where we are amazed and excited by what God is doing, rather than by *our* activities and initiatives. The growth at Greenford has not been by our might or power, but by God's Holy Spirit (Zech 4:6). The glory for growth at Greenford belongs to God alone.

We face an unknown future with a sense of excitement and trepidation at what God – not we – will do.

4

Grosvenor Church, Barnstaple

Dick Chamings

The son of members of Grosvenor Street Chapel, Dick was brought up at Barnstaple, but taught for six years in north London, before returning to north Devon. For fifteen years part of the leadership of a small country church, Dick returned in 1987 to Grosvenor Street Chapel where he has been an elder for the past ten years, and is now church secretary of Grosvenor Church.

Barnstaple nestles in the valley of the river Taw, seven miles from the river's mouth, and has a population of approximately 20,000. It is the administrative, commercial and agricultural centre of North Devon. It is purported to be the oldest (probably one of many!) borough in the country. Our church building, into which we moved in December, 1994, is strategically placed just off the link road that carries heavy traffic from the motorways into North Devon and is almost next door to McDonald's! We are within one or two miles of two large estates.

The church has its roots in work begun by Robert Chapman, who came to Barnstaple in 1832 to become the pastor of Ebenezer Baptist Church. When his ministry at Ebenezer came to an end, ten years later, he sought a site for a new building and by 1848 Grosvenor Street Chapel was completed, although it was known for many years simply as 'The Room'.

RECENT DEVELOPMENTS

The church went through a difficult time during the 1970s and early '80s, and the elders looked to find ways of becoming effective again and reaching out to the community. They invited Dennis Pierce, an evangelist with 'Counties', to take on a part-time pastoral role,

30

which he accepted. It was agreed that, for effective evangelism, times of meeting would need to be changed and a monthly morning family service was introduced.

Dennis eventually moved from Barnstaple to take up his appointment as field secretary of 'Counties'. After his departure, the church began to struggle. Numbers fell gradually. We lost a generation of young people, some to local lively churches. The Sunday evening evangelistic services were often attended by 30 or 40 faithful members with rarely a non-Christian present. Our experience during the time that Dennis had been with us led us to the conviction that we needed someone to be a full-time elder and pastor.

In 1986, Paul Lynch was invited, straight from Bible college, to come and work full-time in the church. Changes continued to be made in the pattern and structure of church activities. More and more use was made of the varied musical skills in the church, and worship became increasingly prominent. Home groups began to meet regularly and the church saw a period of growth. Many people were converted, baptised and joined the fellowship. The Sunday school began to grow again and our services were filled with a spirit of expectancy that God would bless. It soon became evident that a second pastor was needed, and Graham Poland came to us in 1989. We thank God for his gifts as a skilled Bible teacher and leader, and for his vision.

When Paul Lynch left us to to lead a church in Bournemouth, God indicated to us through a vision that he would raise up from within the fellowship someone to take Paul's place. Harry Gillick had become a Christian just a few years before and was soon to retire from the RAF. As we waited on the Lord for guidance, it became more and more obvious to us that here was his man. Harry had the heart of an evangelist and he became responsible for a 'Discovery Group'. When people began to show interest in coming to Christ, but needed time to consider, they would be invited to the home of Harry and Yvonne, where they would explore topics such as 'Why God made me', 'What went wrong with the world?', 'Who Jesus is', and 'How to be born again'. Many people have come to faith through these courses and have gone on to Harry's foundation classes where they were taught further truths about their new faith. Often, when the courses finished, the group had so grown to love each other that they did not want to stop meeting and became a home group.

We are grateful to God that he had raised up a group of elders who did not succumb to the lie, 'We cannot afford it!' At times their decisions seemed reckless, as we were never a rich church and our church giving seemed modest. They decided, too, that other giving, for example to missions, should not be curtailed for any reason. God has always proved faithful and our needs have always been provided.

NEW PREMISES

By now, we were beginning to experience problems with our accommodation. The church was being regularly filled for our Sunday morning family service. Parking was a problem and surveyors' reports were telling us that the church was becoming an increasingly dangerous place to be in. The balcony was put out of action and that part of the building had to be shored up by scaffolding. Our Sunday morning services were for a time held in the local cinema. After a while we returned to the church and held two Sunday morning services. For some time, the elders had considered it necessary either to rebuild or relocate. The collapsing fabric simply helped them decide!

At this time we had no building fund but, after exploring a number of possibilities over a period of two years, the elders met one Saturday in the shell of the old Great Western Railway shed for prayer and to seek guidance. An anonymous gift that very morning of £1000 seemed to confirm the conviction that this was the place where the Lord wanted us to be. This almost derelict building, which had been empty for over two years, had been on the market for £250,000. The company owning it had gone into liquidation at about this time and so we arranged to meet the receiver in Bristol, and made an offer of £75,000 (which we didn't have!). He said that we would need to double the figure for our offer to be considered, but we felt that we should first of all increase the offer to £105,000. (We didn't have that either!) To our surprise he accepted the offer. Unknown to us at the time, the leaseholder had several years left on his lease and was relieved to pay us £35,000 to be released from his obligations. So in effect, we had the whole site, including car parking for well over 100 cars, for £70,000, which was less than the original offer. The church members were invited to view the site. The responses ranged from excitement to 'You have bitten off more than you can chew this time.' With two weeks to go to the completion date, we were still about £50,000 short of the purchase price. The church was informed. We prayed and had a gift day when the target figure was met with almost £10,000 surplus to begin the conversion work. The money was spent on a new roof.

FINANCIAL PROVISION

That was the beginning. The months following have been an exercise of faith which the Lord has honoured. We can see his hand at work achieving things above anything that we could ask or think. The bulk of the money we needed has come through direct giving by members of the fellowship, although a few trusts have given generous donations. On at least five occasions, large bills needed to be paid when there was no money in the bank to pay them. The church was called to pray and fast, and the Lord provided. General giving has also increased significantly during this period.

There have been a number of occasions, too, when God has provided in totally unexpected ways. For example, we received 23 internal door sets from a cancelled order from a local factory. Later we learned that these doors had been ordered for one of her Majesty's prisons! There was a lot of discussion about where the one bullet proof door should be sited: we think that one of the pastors has it! When we moved from the old church our church mini-bus was nearing the end of its life and had to be disposed of. We prayed that the Lord would provide our need. He did so in an interesting way. The County Council contacted us and asked if they could park some of their welfare vehicles on the church site. This was agreed and, in return, they have supplied us with a fleet of mini-buses, and drivers, for the women's work and occasional use for youth work. In lieu of rental they have now completely tarmacked the church car park. This would have cost us many thousands of pounds and certainly would not have been on our list of priorities for many years to come. We thank God for his faithfulness.

A senior elder returned from a term of missionary work just in time to head up the building programme. Endowed with singular administrative and planning skills, a Caleb type of energy, and not a little practical expertise – he was a school teacher before he retired! –

he has superintended the whole building programme and we thank God for him.

At the time of writing we are engaged on the final stage of the development which will provide us with accommodation for a creche, mothers and toddlers groups, Sunday school classes and a large youth lounge.

CHURCH MEMBERSHIP

There has been some growth in our church membership over the past five years. Membership stood at 162 in 1993 and had grown to 255 in 1998. Thirty-three per cent of that increase came through conversion, fifty-five per cent through transfer from other churches, and twelve per cent through re-awakening of faith. We have approximately twenty people between the ages of 18 and 25, sixty between 25 and 40 years, one hundred and ten between 40 and 60 years, and sixty over the age of 60. It is difficult to account for this growth. We look upon it as a gift from a beneficent God and we thank him for the sovereign, renewing work of his Holy Spirit. However, there are features that God has chosen to honour.

DISCOVERY GROUPS

We praise God for the large number of people who have come to Christ through Discovery Groups. Here the gospel is introduced in the most gentle manner, and members of the group are able to talk freely and express doubts and ask questions in a totally non-threatening environment.

SUNDAY SERVICES

Our Sunday morning services give priority to preaching, and regularly provide opportunities for those who are not yet Christians to be made aware of the gospel in a non-threatening atmosphere, using a multi-media approach. We encourage all Christians to develop relationships with those who are unfamiliar with church and invite them on Sunday mornings. However, God moves in mysterious ways! Very recently, a man who lives locally and was at the end of his tether, felt himself drawn to the church. He arrived at the church after the service had ended and was converted in the foyer!

The Sunday evening services are for worship and teaching and normally give opportunities for all Christians to take part. We welcome the exercise of all spiritual gifts, subject to the lordship of Christ and the direction and authority of the church leadership, and for a number of years we have encouraged women to take part in worship and prayer and to exercise their gifts.

PRAYER

We consistently teach the importance of persistent prayer, encouraging the fellowship to pray without ceasing – in home groups, through the telephone prayer chain ministry, through the ministry of our intercessors group, and through corporate times with the whole church. One day we will really believe that prayer changes things!

PREACHING

We set great store by the faithful preaching of God's word. We have always aimed to be systematic and relevant, believing that we need to scratch where people are itching. For example, we have conducted series with themes like 'How to turn your house into a home', 'Christianity on Trial', 'Life's Highway Code', 'Happy ever after?' Determined to meet the varied needs of the fellowship, for a while we provided teaching options in our Sunday evening service. After a time of worship, the congregation were given a choice of two subjects – one devotional and the other practical. The writer looks back on that time with a certain gratitude. One evening his wife chose, rather than listen to him preach on the book of Jeremiah, to hear our financial expert talk on the Christian and his money. She came out from that meeting determined to invest in a 'Save as you earn' scheme that had been recommended. We look forward to its maturing in a few months' time!

TRAINING

For a time, we conducted a Christian Training School considering themes such as 'A Journey through the Bible', 'Know what you believe', 'Worship and Prayer', 'Leadership Skills', 'Learning from the Past'.

FAMILIES

The church recognises its responsibility to the families of those who belong to the church. It aims to support parents in the evangelism and teaching of their children. It recognises that young people need to be discipled in the context of their peer group, and to be given reasons for believing in an environment that is free from pressure, so that they may grow and maintain a witness among their non-Christian friends in the secular atmosphere of their schools. To this end the church provides Sunday and mid-week activities for all age ranges, our youth coordinator implementing the policy.

The fact that we have a splendid building so close to major roads, local estates and McDonald's cannot be ignored! People seem to appreciate its convenience and are grateful that they know they will be able to park their car. Because of the nearness to the local estates, we are able to run successful mother and toddler groups for three sessions each week and still have a waiting list of some 50 families. We run two outreach children's clubs with about 200 children on the books, and a successful meeting for older women.

DISCIPLESHIP

However, we have been challenged in the past two years to consider our priorities. We realised that we had been an activity-based church, the important consideration being 'What do we do?' Our concept of the church fellowship was based on the activities that took place during the week, and so we had become very building-centred. God has challenged us to review, not so much what we *do* but who we *are* – being rather than doing. We needed, badly, to build up relationships with one another. Our premises would be used to meet that end.

At about this time, our senior pastor took a sabbatical and spent some time in Brazil observing what God was doing there. He discovered that one of the key factors in the rapid growth of the church in that country was the rediscovery of the importance of discipleship through relationships. He came back convinced that this was what God intended for us. Then followed a period of intensive teaching, prayer and discussion. We discovered – or should we say re-discovered – that discipleship through relationship is New Testament Christianity. It was the model used by Jesus and is best achieved in small groups or one-to-one. Jesus taught through relating to his disciples; he shared his life with them. For over three years they were with him, travelling and living together. They heard him speak, saw him work, watched him perform tasks. They watched him die. Jesus was their model to follow.

We took as our foundation stones two scriptures: Jesus' commission, 'Go and make disciples of all nations, baptising them in the name of the Father and of the Son and of the Holy Spirit, and teaching them to obey everything that I have commanded you.' (Matt 28:16–20); and Paul's word to Timothy, 'And the things you have heard me say in the presence of many witnesses entrust to reliable men who will also be qualified to teach others.' (2 Tim 2:2)

Discipleship, we decided, requires that we pass on to others what God is doing in our lives and they, in turn, pass it on to others. We share what we learn; we do not keep it to ourselves. Our goal will always be to become like Jesus. Three principles would be adopted that would mark us out as disciples of Jesus:

DYING TO SELF

1. We would be prepared to die to ourselves. (Luke 14:25–33)
This would prove to be a painful process. To 'die to self' would involve such things as dying to our pride and reputation, being vulnerable with other people and being prepared to let Jesus change us. We needed to understand what D L Moody meant when he said, 'Beware of the man who has nothing to lose.' If we had died, then we would have nothing to lose. We would do everything Jesus said and it would not matter if we looked foolish or revealed our personal weaknesses, because we would have nothing to lose. When we began to share with others about our struggles or our needs we

invited them to help us and to share in our struggles. As we revealed our needs others felt needed and they would reach out and support us and love us, because the atmosphere of love is produced through an atmosphere of brokenness.

LOVING ONE ANOTHER

2. We would love our fellow Christians. (John 13:34,35)
Jesus began to say to us in a new way that if we wanted to be his disciples then we needed to love one another, and that love would be a product not only of brokenness but also of an action of the will. In the context of our small groups we would have an opportunity to serve one another through love. In the past, when we met in small groups the emphasis had been on the 'meeting'. Now the emphasis would be on the 'people', and we would need to learn to love the people in our group in whatever way they needed. By being part of a small group we would be committing ourselves to love and be loved. Discipleship groups would be our family where we could be accepted, encouraged and protected, and have the security of knowing who is responsible for us.

SUBMITTING TO AUTHORITY

3. We would submit to authority and discipline. (Heb 13:17)
Jesus told his followers that discipleship meant teaching them to obey 'everything I have commanded you'. Those who are put over us in the Lord would be trusted with the task of ensuring that we understood and followed what Jesus had laid down in his word.

WORKING IT OUT

But how would this all work out in practice? We are still very much in the learning stages. We have amended our mission statement which now reads: 'Through a process of discipleship, we aim to bring those who are not yet Christians into an intimate relationship with God through Christ and into intimate relationships with other Christians.' The main reason why God has left us as Christians here on earth is that we might be lights in the darkness and that we might build relationships with those who are not yet Christians and bring them into what we have found. As a church our primary focus is that, as a people of God, we might be a light set in the darkness – and it will continue to be a priority. It is not enough to see people making decisions to become Christians and come along to church; that is not our full aim. This is that those who do not know Jesus yet might be brought beyond a decision to a process of discipleship where they enter into a relationship with God which is intimate. That is what we are about as Christians, coming into that close relationship with God through Jesus. But it cannot stop there. From there, we want to develop intimate relationships with each other in such a way that, just as we get to know God intimately, so in the same way we might start to get to know each other, support each other, disciple each other and lead each other into all that God has for us.

So we say to new Christians and newcomers to the church: 'Everyone wanting to be part of Grosvenor Church is encouraged to participate in a process of discipleship through relationship. One person will be attached to you and then you will become part of a small group. In order to maintain the biblical model of 2 Timothy 2:2, everyone needs to be in relationship two ways: to receive discipling and support; and to pass on what they have received. Therefore, at some stage in the future we would hope that you, in turn, would be able and willing to disciple others.'

If only we could say that all this has been plain sailing! Some people have said in effect, 'We do not want to go down this road', and have become part of the one hundred folk who meet with us on a Sunday morning but who are not part of the discipling pattern. Others have said, 'We will go along with you but have serious reservations.' Sadly, some have left us and gone elsewhere. Others do not understand the decreasing emphasis on 'church services', even though we still meet together every Sunday morning and two Sunday evenings each month.

Too Much Activity

To these people we are gently trying to say that one of the barriers to developing relationships is too much activity. Martin Luther King used to pray, 'Lord, give me time to love.' We say that relationships are built, gifts are discovered and developed, discipline is exercised, worship and teaching take place in the context of the small group, and we think that this is biblical. We say that the church building is a marvellous resource given by God to reach the people all around who are lost, but it is only a tool, a facility we can use in order to build people into living relationships.

CONGREGATION AND CELL

We have turned the concept of congregation and cell on its head. We now say that the congregation is the stepping stone to the cell or small group, rather than the reverse. The aim of Christian fellowship is not that we 'go to church' with a large group of people and then go home but that, out of the large group, we might be funnelled into a small group where we really get to grips with what the Bible is saying about relationship and growing.

Some have said that we have done too much too quickly. On reflection, this may be the case and we are endeavouring to restate the vision regularly, encourage deeper relationships between the leaders – we now have about fifty people who lead discipleship groups – and meet with the people who are confused or critical in order to confront the issues. Others have been concerned that they had not been successfully 'kept in the picture'.

COMMUNICATING THE VISION

We are still learning how difficult it is to maintain good communications in a fairly large church. For a long period, we held what we called 'Vision and Communication Nights' at which we kept the church up-to-date with all matters relating to our church life. We are now relying on the leaders of the discipleship groups to be the main channel of information to the fellowship.

THE FUTURE

The two pastors and six elders will continue to meet each week for prayer, and twice a month to discuss business and pastoral issues.

They will continue to seek God because they realise there is still so much to learn and do. They all need to become what Peter Wagner would call 'possibility thinkers', men who believe in a great God who is still able to break through into our community in the power of his Holy Spirit and make a difference. We humbly thank God for what he has done and are excited about what he is going to do.

5

Maghull Chapel, Merseyside: Starting from scratch (well almost)

John Knipe

*'Never out of a Brethren assembly', John has been successively
elder in two churches since 1952 (now emeritus). Maghull Chapel
was born in his home and he was one of the two prime movers.
After serving in the police for 25 years, he worked nearly as long
as a solicitor's managing clerk. Now aged 77, John is 'still
working hard'.*

Maghull is a dormitory town eleven miles north of the centre of
Liverpool, separated from the city by a narrow green belt which con-
tains, among other things, the famous Grand National race course at
Aintree.

Forty years ago, the area was fertile agricultural land which still
grows the finest potatoes and barley in Britain. However, most of
the area is now covered with modern semis. With a few exceptions,
the houses are modest, owner-occupied, good quality homes.

CHURCH GROWTH

About thirty years ago, a small group of Christians, members of
'Brethren' assemblies in Liverpool but living in Maghull, met to discuss the planting of a 'New Testament church' nearer their homes.
That title was used because it was felt that they would bring with
them the best of their background and leave behind those things
which they thought were perhaps unhelpful. The result was a
church with a very 'open' attitude.

There followed a steering committee; a weekly prayer meeting in
the garage of a house which also served as Citizens Advice Bureau;

42

then a Sunday school in a local school building. From the start this was a great success, with 93 children on the first Sunday and rapid growth thereafter. Next came a mixed Covenanter group and a large youth group, mainly of sixth formers, who called themselves 'Group 4' (They had four aims, one of which was security!)

The fellowship itself grew apace, probably because of its unusually open attitude in a group of churches which some folk were beginning to feel were becoming too legalistic.[1]

Eventually this growing group of believers left their home assemblies and began to break bread together in Maghull, in the home of one of their number. There was great hope, faith and enthusiasm among them.

A BUILDING TO MEET IN

A hunt was instituted for land that greedy builders might have missed. A paddock was found, which boasted an old garage and a donkey, but the owner was not willing to sell. He was given a contact name, address and telephone number, and we prayed. Eventually he got in touch. The group bought his land but, unhappily, the donkey had gone, which was such a pity because he could have been useful at Christmas! Christians over a wide area prayed and gave or loaned money, and they started to build.

They hired two bricklayers and a labourer, and paid them per thousand bricks they laid. The Lord sent to the fellowship people with building qualifications and skills – and some with just muscle – and each weeknight (with the exception of prayer meeting night) and all day Saturday, they laboured, often in deep mud. In three years and three months, they had adorned the land with a pleasing modern building. Finance came in at about the speed they were able to build.

They called the building Maghull Chapel. It has an auditorium which can seat about 180 persons. There are three large rooms and a kitchen, and at the moment there is a planning application before the local council for 'change of use' of the house next door. We are growing a little faster than the natural wastage.

---

1. G C D Howley was among those who were warning of this at the time. See *A New Testament Church in 1955 (NTC)*, the report of the High Leigh Conference of Brethren held in September 1955 (privately printed) p 21. Every church overseer should read this document.

A Setback

At one stage, we lost twenty-five people, mainly young, in a charismatic breakaway, which we might have handled better – but there were some hard heads in both camps. Those who left were some of our best people, ready to stand up and be counted, workers among the young, not afraid of knocking on doors, and rarely missing from the prayer meeting. They were a great loss to us. They formed the Maghull Christian Fellowship and we have a good relationship with them today. They meet in a school and we loan them our building for baptisms. They have grown and have recently taken over a church which seemed about to close, four miles away in Thornton.

Recovery

We soon made up the loss and grew further. Today we have about 117 adult and young adult believers in the Maghull Chapel fellowship. We do not keep records, or a diary of comings and goings, or statistics of any kind. Today few have 'Brethren' backgrounds – perhaps about twenty families – and we have dropped the 'Brethren' tag. We never started with it anyway, and early 'Brethren' over 160 years ago did not want it either: like them we were given it by others.

Many have been saved among us, some with unfortunate and unhappy backgrounds. In some cases, this is the only church they have ever experienced. For them it is an adventure they never dreamed existed and there are now inexperienced evangelists galore (only a slight exaggeration!) In this last twelve months or so, the church has developed, quite unconsciously, an ethos of reaping. We are preparing for our fourth Alpha course. People have joined us, having moved into the town from elsewhere.

Mothers and Toddlers Groups

We have two mothers and toddlers groups (130 children in all) plus grandmas and grandads, mums and dads, and professional child minders. Not long ago we nearly closed both groups because we said that they took a great deal out and put nothing in. (Week by week, they put nappies down the loos, blocking the drains and driving us round the bend!) A couple of years ago, we appointed a full-time evangelist and, about the same time, the deputy head of a big inner city school, an overseer on sabbatical, took early retirement. Between them, they took over mums and tots. The prayers of the women workers and of the church were heard in heaven and now we are reaping in that area. The tide has turned. There is a Bible time input in both groups.

FAMILY SERVICE

We have an action-packed, well attended family service run by a small team of men and women who, though already skilled, have recently had some training.

LUNCHEON CLUB

Our weekly old folks' luncheon club is 35 to 45 strong, and we also have a coffee shop. People have come to Christ through both. We have been surprised at the number of people, young and old, who are desperately lonely today.

KEEP FIT

An evening keep fit class for women meets the needs of those not fit enough to run away! Homemakers is a monthly outreach to women and, because they talk about rings and bracelets and clothing and other expensive items, the men have dubbed it 'Homewreckers'! The building is open for some activity or other five days a week and often seven.

YOUTH WORK

We do not have the large Sunday school and youth groups we once had, but we are glad to report that work among young people is starting to grow again – not necessarily on a Sunday. We touch eighty children in a week overall, and the number is growing. We send more children to Merseyside Christian Youth Camps (an 'assemblies' initiative) than anyone else; a position we hold jointly with another church. We have young people away at college or university, some of whom are really making their mark.

Community Recognition

Our outreach into the community has been appreciated by the local authority. They sent one of their officers to look us over and later, without our asking, they sent us over £2000, with which we refurbished the kitchen. 'The Lord knows those things ye have need of.'

A Full-time Evangelist

Geoff Ardern is our salaried full-time evangelist. We were slow to take the step of appointing him, despite the fact that the Lord was telling us we should. We felt we could not afford it, but we read or were told a number of times by people who had passed that way before us: 'Appoint someone and the money will come.' That has proved true for us as well.

Geoff functions as evangelist, encourager and ideas man. He has a pastor's heart and does some shepherding. In two local schools he is as welcome as the staff, and takes assemblies every week. We have a cash input into those schools annually for the purchase of good quality Christian books for use by the RE teachers, under the Stapleford Project. They think highly of Geoff – and so do we. We are also glad of the input of Brenda, his wife. Geoff was appointed by a decision of the whole church.

Growth

There has been natural wastage over the years, but always enough growth to keep abreast of the loss and eventually overtake it. Most of the fellowship live within walking distance of the church. The pedestrian and car traffic in and out are a good advertisement. A local, trying to block one of our planning applications, wrote: 'It's more like a community centre than a church.' We think that is more of a commendation than a condemnation. We have married and buried some people who were not in the fellowship. People have told us that they felt a warmth of love when they first arrived that they had not experienced before, and we have been told by visitors on a number of occasions: 'We felt God was here.'

LEADERSHIP

In the matter of church government, the two oldest overseers here, without being asked, took the advice of the late beloved Harold St John given at the 1955 conference already mentioned. When asked what should be done about an elder whose powers are waning, the advice was given: 'Allow him to act as a sort of emeritus professor, giving him still the opportunity of doing what he can while, at the same time, he will learn to grow old gracefully' (*NTC*, page 52). Here, they advise and assist when asked, but are not involved in the day-to-day running and decision-making of the church.

We are sometimes asked why we are growing despite the natural wastage, when other churches are in decline. One of the answers is that some years ago the overseers decided that they would meet every Monday evening specifically for prayer for the church. The writer believes that God honoured that commitment to prayer, for from then onward there was gradual change and growth which, in the main, has been almost painless.

The church leaders have spent time and prayer on these matters at home and on 'away days'. They have read what has been written in Partnership reports and have had to think and pray through many things. They have been willing to think again after reading books by 'Brethren' authors, for example, *Go tell my Brothers* (Cedric Longville),*Roots, Renewal and the Brethren* (ND Smith), *Declare His Glory* (John Baigent and others), Kevin Dyer's excellent work *Must Brethren Churches Die?* and a book edited by DJ Ellis and WW Gasque, *In God's Community* . They have been willing to change not only their thinking but, if necessary, their practice.

Today we have a leadership team comprising two overseers (we need three) and four co-ordinators, two of whom are godly women with real abilities. Each co-ordinator is responsible for an area of church life, under the guidance of the overseers. Areas are whole church matters; youth and evangelism; administration; pastoral. Each co-ordinator recruits his or her own team to do the Lord's work in the church. This means that a large number of church members are at work in the church, according to their gifting, and as a result the overseers and leaders are not straining under a workload they cannot carry.

In order to help people to discover their gifting, we held a meeting of the whole church at which each was asked to write down what gifts they felt they had, and what gifts they thought other people had. We found a large degree of agreement and later used people in the area where their gifts lay. On the whole, the system is working well.

The church reveals a cross-section of the community in which we work. We have not been immune from the problems of redundancy and unemployment; we have people on supplementary benefits; and one-parent families with the distress that brings with it. In the writer's view the backbone of the church is the 'middle marrieds'. They are the most marvellous group of dedicated workers you could wish for, and they work hand-in-hand with the singles without whom the church would be much the poorer.

The normal church activities include Coffee Shop, Keep Fit Group, Homemakers, and Ladies' Meeting. The Lord has blessed us with gift and expertise. A dinner for sixty can be produced at any time. 'Impact' (the Merseyside expression of Partnership) has been quick to harness that potential in order to bring church leaders together to build relationships rather than for preaching.

We have a sprinkling of professional people who get on well with our old age pensioners and artisans of all kinds. We are not so 'way out' as to deter intelligent professionals from joining us, nor are we so devoid of the Spirit's fire that people with a charismatic bent will not feel at home among us. Spiritual gifts are in evidence, and teaching has been given on that subject.

ROLE OF WOMEN

The overseers prayed and looked afresh at the position of women in the church in the light of the scriptures. Rightly believing that they had the confidence of the church, they released women to pray in the prayer meeting, and told the church that they could see no bar to their praying in any meeting, but felt it would be too big a step to include the communion service at that time. The church accepted that and, some time later, released them to pray in any meeting.[2] When that happened, one older couple with a strict background left the fellowship. Today, in 1998, women have liberty at all meetings to pray and express their thoughts on scripture. They are not involved in the authoritative teaching of the word, though we realise the line between the two is a fine one. We have no problems yet, on this matter.

MUSIC

Another reason for growth is music. People will come because they like the music. But how do you meet a cross-section of tastes in the community such as we have? We do our best! Music is a very delicate, yet a very important area because 'God inhabits the praises of his people'. Some years ago we invited a team from Gold Hill Baptist Church in Berkshire, itself a growing church, to come and take a look at us to see if they could criticise and help us. This was then the Rev Jim Graham's church, one of those commemorated in the book, *Ten Growing Churches*. They were a great help in this area, and a number of others. One of the things they said was that because music was an area at the heart of worship and this was so important to God then, if the Devil was going to launch an attack, it would probably involve the music group. That has proved correct.

We use a clavinova (an electrical instrument which plays piano and organ music) and strings. Some musicians use their own electronic keyboards, guitars, flutes and drums, rarely all at one time. Every ear, young and old, whatever the taste, gets a turn – even the deaf can hear! We use the clavinova at the communion service. There is some clapping and hands raised heavenward when the words and music are appropriate.

PREACHERS

What about preachers? We took note of the late Prof FF Bruce's warning: 'We greatly overdo this peripatetic ministry.'[3] We

2. See G C D Howley's comments in *NTC*, p 41.
3. *NTC*, p 52.

stopped inviting preachers for some time and gave our own men a chance to try their gift in a friendly atmosphere. We suffered a little occasionally, but have grown a small crop of acceptable preachers.

COMMUNION

The reader will probably ask about our communion service because it rightly lies at the heart of our tradition. Our attitude is the same as that of the late beloved Harold St John (1955 Conference, page 88) 'I find in reading the writings of our beloved brother Paul that he places the whole burden of responsibility for "breaking bread" squarely and solely on the shoulders of the one who wishes to do so. We are not told he has to be interrogated or examined ... '[4] Our experience has been that folk have broken bread with us and, when visited after some weeks, have trusted the Lord and stayed with us.

The service for breaking of bread lasts a little over forty-five minutes. Sometimes we hit the high spots and praise soars heavenward but, because we are human, the service is occasionally mediocre. We are working on that one. Visitors have said they have appreciated the spontaneous praise and worship.

We have never made baptism a requirement for participation, having taken the view of earlier 'Brethren' that 'life' and not 'light' was the factor to be considered. We do, of course, teach and practise believers' baptism.

PRAYER

Prayer meetings are about forty strong and Geoff has recently shaken us up in that area. Care groups account for a further thirty praying people and there are some prayer triplets. God listens to us and we listen to him. We try to obey him and we have a willingness to change which we believe is a further reason for growth.

---

4. *NTC*, p 88.

FINANCE

As to finance, we have an annual budget of about £35,000 and we are working on that too.

FUTURE

We have a vision to plant a number of neighbourhood groups across the area by the year 2000, probably in homes. One of them has already been started on a problem estate in the home of a newly converted woman who is an enthusiastic witness for Jesus.

REACTIONS IN THE CHURCH

Sometimes there has been a little unease as changes have been made. However, it has been a joy and a confirmation to discover from Partnership reports that 'Brethren' churches in other parts of the country have followed a similar road with similar results. On the very day the then leaders met to discuss team leadership, the current edition of *Partnership Perspectives* arrived, containing reports on that subject from churches elsewhere in the country. We were grateful for the confirmation.

RELATIONSHIPS WITH OTHER CHURCHES

Another reason the writer believes the Lord has blessed us with growth is that from very early days we respected the unity of the Body of Christ. For example, before we started a Sunday school the ministers of other churches were visited and told that we were not in competition but would strive together with them for the faith of the gospel. Today we meet regularly with other church leaders. We have a vision to visit every house in the town with a copy of a gospel before the year 2000 and to double the 'congregation' by then. We realise we cannot do that alone. 'Brethren' and 'suchlike' churches must, we believe, learn that they cannot win their area for Christ on their own. Here, we work well with the evangelical churches and do the best we can with the rest. We hope they learn something from our zeal.

On a recent 'World Day of Prayer' the united prayer meeting was held at our church and one of two nuns said to me: 'We pass your church every Sunday and love to hear the wonderful singing.' (We didn't realise we were so good!)

WORLD MISSION

We have to confess to not being a very missionary orientated church, perhaps because we have been so busy at home. This matter may need some attention -though 20% of our offerings go to missionaries or missionary organisations working across the globe.

We made the mistake of sending one of our prettiest girls to Operation Mobilisation's Luke Training Centre at Halesowen where, among other things, she learned how to be a clown (without a lot of effort we may add!) and a very good communicator to young people. Almost inevitably, a young Italian male 'OMer' fell in love with her and we married them here in 1997. They are not starting a circus, as far as we know, and we will let you pray for Rachel and Giuseppe, if you wish, as they now work full-time by faith for the Lord in Italy.

* * * * * * * * *

GEOFF GOES TO SCHOOL

'Hi! Geoff here. John has mentioned the Stapleford scheme through which a church or group of churches can adopt a school and provide teaching materials for teaching Christianity under the RE Syllabus. The sponsorship offer (£200 per school per annum) was warmly received by the two local primary schools close to the chapel and complemented my weekly visits to both schools to take assemblies.

The school contact is both stretching and fruitful. There is regular opportunity to make input into the lives of 500 children aged 4 to 11 years with a lot of fun, but side issues, beneficial to all parties, are developing nicely.

The familiar face of the man who takes a weekly assembly at their school is a very convenient contact when, under the RE banner, they need to visit 'a place of worship'. So, several times, children from both schools have seen around Maghull Chapel and been told of the activities run each week, with accompanying parents (necessary for safety) listening. A couple of weeks ago, a mother said to me at the end of such a visit: 'So you're Mr Ardern. My child often comes home singing a song or quoting the story, and I wondered who this person was.' An unscheduled assembly during an OFSTED visit gave the school an opportunity to show their contact with the community.

The end of the school year gives the opportunity to present each school leaver (junior department) with a Scripture Union booklet *Moving On*, which is well received.

There are the odd invitations to school performances at Christmas, Easter and Harvest and, at the time of writing, one of the best invitations yet: to be asked to take the funeral of the mother of the school secretary, whose office door adjacent to the school hall is left open during assembly. The request for a funeral suggests a memorial service at Maghull Chapel. So another home is brought to hear of a loving Jesus. They have never been before, and my guess is they'll come again. We'll see.

Yours, Geoff'

* * * * * * * * * *

CONCLUSION

God has allowed us to make mistakes. We have not got it all right, but we are working hard on it. By the world's standards we are a small church struggling with many problems as we reach into the community for our beloved Lord.

Not everyone with a 'Brethren' background would be happy among us, but people are coming, hearing the gospel and finding the Saviour. In addition, we have 'a good report from those who are without'.

We are trying to leave the next generation a vibrant, living faith rather than a dead orthodoxy – just as those old 'Brethren' leaders said at the High Leigh conference in 1955.

It costs . . . but it's worth it'.

6
Nant Coch Church, Newport, South Wales
Gill Capper

Gill Capper took early retirement after 30 years as a lecturer in a college of further education. She spends much of her time as a member of the Magistrates' Bench and several magistrates' committees. An active member of Nant Coch, she is connected with various Christian organisations (including Partnership). She has been associated with the Women's Bible Study Conference for many years and has recently helped to set up a similar venture in Wales. She also enjoys visiting groups in many parts of Wales and the West Country, speaking, teaching and encouraging women in their Christian lives. What follows is Gill's personal assessment of her church.

OUR MISSION STATEMENT

By proclamation and demonstration of the truth of Christ's message, to increase the membership of the Church local and world-wide and to encourage every member to grow in Christian character and in the knowledge of God.

PAST

In the early years of the war, Newport (then in Monmouthshire) became one of the principal embarkation ports for soldiers on their way to France and beyond. Members of a large assembly in the town set up a work to minister to the men as they waited to leave. They rented a shop unit in the centre of town which was converted into what they called the 'Soldiers' Rest'. Here they could sit and talk, drink tea, write letters and be cared for by Christians. Stephen Olford, with his parents, had settled in the town, living in the missionary home run by the assembly. His tremendous evangelistic talents were encouraged and developed by my father, John Capper, and other Christians in the area, and his work with the troops was very fruitful.

In 1942 a number of families left the local assembly to form a new and more open fellowship in a school in a different part of the town and this eventually became known as Nant Coch (Welsh for 'red stream') after the name of the house in which the school was operating. The work with the soldiers and the formation of a Young People's Christian Fellowship made an impact on the town, and another school was rented for Sunday evening services. These were timed to coincide with the ending of the majority of Sunday evening services so that many from various denominations came. The programme was lively, and the emphasis was on evangelism. All this was quite revolutionary.

Stephen Olford functioned for some time in a semi-official capacity as 'pastor' of this new and outward-looking fellowship. He went on to become pastor of Duke Street Baptist Church, Richmond and then to Calvary Baptist Church in New York and a worldwide evangelistic and teaching ministry. This has been well documented in his biography *Only one Life*, written by John Phillips, former assistant director of Moody Correspondence School and Emmaus Correspondence School, who also had strong connections with Nant Coch as his parents lived at the missionary home in Newport for some time.

In the early 1950s the church, now meeting in a room in a private house, started to search for a permanent home. A large house in the same area as Nant Coch House was considered, and eventually purchased for £1800. In recent years there have been many changes. The service in the town centre school continued with great blessing until around 1970 when it was moved to the Nant Coch church building and became their evening service. In 1981 the meeting room accommodation had become much too small, and a large hall was built on. This was a great time of growth for the church. Situated in the centre of a community with many children and young people, there was much interest in Sunday school and youth work, as well as the Bible studies and women's Bible study group.

PRESENT

Since this major building programme, a number of further projects have been undertaken and at the present time building work is in progress to create a large room for our young people's group, enlarge the kitchen and bring other facilities into line with modern health, safety and hygiene regulations.

As far as numbers go, we have approximately 160 committed members and an enormous fringe. We have three different congregations – on Sunday morning and Sunday evening, and at the family service held on the first Sunday of each month – with some people coming to only one of those services. Recently we have had a paid part-time youth worker who proved to be a great success. She returned to Romania where she was working for two years prior to her year at Nant Coch. She has now been replaced with a full-time youth worker who is already making a most valuable contribution to that area of the church's work.

As far as the leadership is concerned, there are six elders and, until recently, four deacons. However the church is in the process of re-structuring the leadership and looking at gifting within the fellowship. A series of seminars is involving the membership in full consultation. We have had a considerable amount of help from Partnership churches who have been good enough to describe and be really honest about church structures in the pages of *Partnership Perspectives*. We have also found Jonathan Lamb's booklet *Making Progress in Church Life* helpful as we looked at the process of change within the fellowship.

Basically, the work of the church has been grouped into five sections – main meetings; youth and children; mission worldwide and evangelism; pastoral care and discipleship training; practical and support. Each is under the leadership of a co-ordinator. A sixth section and what is, at the present time, known as the Acts 6:4 group will have the burden for vision, prayer, teaching planning, ministry and membership matters. Yes – they will be elders in function but we have resisted the temptation to spend hours discussing nomenclature.

How can I describe the activities of the fellowship? The planning group identified about fifty and then, when we received responses from individuals recently, we were reminded of even more! The regular programme of church activities follows the general pattern of other fellowships. There are three services on Sundays. The communion is followed by a short service which is called 'Prime Time'. The young people and members of Sunday club are in their own rooms and the service in the main hall is just 35–40 minutes long. Parents bring their children to the Sunday club and are encouraged to stay. The evening service is well attended and has a varied programme. Once a month we have a morning family service which is always well attended, numbers sometimes reaching more than 200. This has provided us with a great opportunity.

During the week there are Bible study groups – one in the church building itself and others in homes. Generally they work through the same material so that if someone can't join a group on a Tuesday for some reason, they can join a Wednesday group instead. There are other groups – for men a 'Discovery Bible Study', for women a 'What's in the Bible?' group, and for younger women a group (with creche facilities) which is at present joining an Alpha group in another church in the town. A large part of the church's pastoral care and teaching is done within these groups but for those who for many reasons are not or will not be in a group, some provision is made – quite a challenge!

A major development in the life of the church was the introduction of a group for mothers and toddlers. This has been running for some years and has proved so popular that there are two groups, and sometimes the long waiting list has had to be closed. Many people have been contacted as a result of this group, and we thank God for those who have gradually started attending services, some of whom have joined study groups and eventually have come to know the Lord.

A large number of children who began as members of the toddlers group, graduate to Sunday club and later join the summer holiday club. As a spin-off from the holiday club, a weekly 'Go-for-it' club for children aged 7–11 was formed, and this has been immensely successful although very hard work. There are a number of specialised activities – a service in a nearby residential nursing home and, in particular, a Bible study and home interest group for Japanese women. There are a number of Japanese companies in the area and through God-given contacts, help with cultural knowledge and advice from a Japanese Christian family, and our own missionaries who work in Japan, this work has been going for some years.

The prayer networks within the fellowship are of vital importance. We have a church prayer and praise meeting once a week, but the work of the church is also backed up by the prayer sessions within the Bible study groups, a very active prayer chain system, special purpose prayer groups and a number of prayer triplet groups which meet regularly. Our young people's group known as 'Grape Vine' organises a 'Prayers on Toast' group which meets very early in the mornings once a week, with all those attending guaranteed transport to school on time. It is this network of prayer which is so vital to all our work. We have found that focused days and times of meeting for prayer have been a tremendous blessing. In 1998, the Evangelical Alliance's 'A Day to Pray' event proved to be a very precious time for us all. The elders and deacons recently held an 'Away Day' to discuss and work through the implications of the new leadership structure plans. While this was going on, church members were in the church premises for six one-hour sessions of prayer for the leaders.

It has been a great experience to build special prayer focus times into the programme. It has become a regular practice to have an evening of prayer on the first Saturday in the new year. This has been a time of great spiritual blessing, thankfulness and dedication for all who are able to attend. The church is realising that when people get together to pray, covenant between each other to pray, make particular focuses on prayer; then things happen. Prayer sessions are run imaginatively, with plenty of variety, purpose and determination. God knits together his people as they work together in prayer – young and old, able and less able, mature Christians and those who have recently become Christians. The joy which is experienced when answers to prayer are made known and shared becomes a witness to the power of prayer within the fellowship. Gone are the days when listeners in the prayer meeting were taken round Africa, India and South America, through most of the Old Testament prophecies, and back via the teachings of some old divine long passed into glory!

As far as missionary work is concerned, over the years a large number of people have gone out into full-time service. Today, a number of overseas workers are being supported by the fellowship in addition to two of our young people who are on overseas mission placement as part of their gap year. On the home front, we have two working in other parts of the country on a full-time basis and one, an associate with Open Air Campaigners, who works full-time in primary schools throughout Gwent. Tony Bugeja has a remarkable ministry. He is invited regularly to almost all the schools in the county of Gwent, and it is estimated that he reaches something like 30,000 children each year. This takes a great deal of organising, support and prayer but we thank God for this tremendous opportunity which is so close to our hearts and the work of the fellowship, town and wider district.

During the year of our fiftieth anniversary, the church set up an 'Investors in People' fund which enables us to give financial support from time to time to those who are involved in special Christian projects. This has proved to be a great encouragement to many and has helped to fund travel and support on a number of occasions.

We have strong links with other churches and fellowships in the area. Our members enjoy going to Spring Harvest and many other camps, week-end houseparties, Graham Kendrick and Steve Chalke events, Keswick convention, Alpha groups, Partnership week-ends and the Women's Bible study conferences. Our membership of the Evangelical Alliance has proved very helpful and informative. A number of members have attended their recent seminars, one encouraging mission and another concerning the implications of the coming Welsh Assembly. Members who are on e-mail keep in regular contact with missionaries and this helps them and us to be able to pray and support imaginatively and quickly.

Yes – we have enormous challenges and some really big problems, and there are always obstacles to distract leaders and other members of the fellowship from being able to get on as they would like. We have had our share of tragic deaths, illnesses, family and marriage problems, unemployment, unfair dismissal and redundancy. The very different problems of the late 1990s have to be faced with renewed courage and wisdom, love and understanding.

Looking at the church as a whole, I would say that it is a lively, warmhearted and loving fellowship; fresh, open and welcoming with a large proportion of members who have come from completely non-Christian backgrounds. The fellowship has a big heart for the needs of the local community and the world. and looks forward to the opportunities which the re-structuring will bring. We are aware of gaps in the programme and activities which must be filled.

FUTURE

One of the main verses which has been used during the preparation of the new leadership structure is Ephesians 4:16: 'From Him the whole body, joined and held together by every supporting ligament, grows and builds itself up in love, as each part does its work.' As we look, pray and prepare for the future, it is essential to look at the whole body and the development of the supporting ligaments. It is the active building up that we must aim at and not just the business of dealing with injury and muscle fatigue.

In recent months, commitment has been the subject of numerous talks and discussions. It is expected that those who are regular members and attenders of the Nant Coch fellowship will consider themselves part of that body and beholden to the church in matters of allegiance and faithfulness.

It is expected that they will be responsible towards other members, joining together in prayer, fellowship, worship and action in the life of the church. They have responsibilities towards each other in matters of care and concern at many different levels. They are developing a strong urge to preach the gospel of Jesus Christ locally and worldwide and to encourage growth in character and knowledge.

If there is to be commitment from members of the fellowship, each member should receive entitlements from their membership. In my view, these include the following:

1. To experience the gospel of Jesus Christ being proclaimed faithfully in a variety of ways on a regular basis. Members must receive constant reminders and teaching about the claims of Christ and the importance and urgency of evangelism.
2. To be encouraged and trained to pass on the good news to others both in the normal services of the church, through special events based at the church or in working with others in larger evangelistic activities. To be encouraged and, where possible, trained to explain the gospel of Jesus Christ, to nurture new Christians and to be part of the work of building up the membership in maturity, and in the knowledge of God.
3. To receive regular teaching on all matters of doctrine, principles and practice of the Christian faith, so that all matters of faith and doctrine are covered in, say, a three- or five-year period.

4. To be prayed for, personally, on a regular basis and to be encouraged to be part of the prayer and intercession activities of the church.

5. Where appropriate, to be encouraged to attend special courses/ seminars, conferences, training days in order to develop individual gifts for use in the fellowship and to develop as members in their own Christian growth. Now that gifts have and are being identified, there must be active work in looking at individuals and seeing where and how skills can be developed. This does not apply just to the young, potential leaders, but to any who need skill development in some particular field.

6. To receive opportunities to train for full-time and part-time Bible study teaching – perhaps with a view to short- or long-term full-time work at home where it is so desperately needed, or overseas. Also to be trained to be able to teach and share the word in our own services and to go out from the church to speak at local churches and meetings.

7. To know and experience love and care given only through Christ, which is the main part of the process of building up the fellowship.To receive prayer and pastoral support. Pastoral help to be available to all on a regular and systematic basis. To be given opportunities to train in pastoral care and in counselling.

8. To be provided with opportunities for fellowship, apart from main meetings for members, and on many occasions, as part of the evangelistic outreach of the fellowship such as social activities.

9. To be able to be part of a prayer triplet, prayer chain or prayer group and to be encouraged to pray systematically for other members, groups, or a particular section of overseas work. To know that all church-based activities will be planned and covered with prayer.

10. To be kept informed of all matters which concern the church at home and worldwide. To be kept informed on current affairs from a Christian point of view. To be kept informed and encouraged to link up with Christians from other fellowships and to know that they are part of the wider church body.

11. To be able to attend and worship in a building which is safe and well maintained. To know that the monetary contributions they make will be spent wisely and responsibly.

12. To be made aware of the vision and goals set by the church lead-

ers and co-ordinators of each group and what their part is in praying for and working towards those goals.

13. To know that the activities of the fellowship are constantly under review and that, under the guidance and authority of the Holy Spirit, the church is being led on fearlessly, to become a vital force within the community and within the totality of the body of Christ.

14. To know that there is an active programme for families within the 3- or 5-year system. At any one time there should be a scheme for families in the plan – including parenting classes (as are now being run), courses for parents of teenagers, parents in pain or suffering from 'empty nest' syndrome. All these should be 'seeded' into the plan so that at the time one course is running, the next is being planned.

15. To have provision for singles in the church who at present constitute about one-third of the membership, with provision for every age group.

16. For every member to be aware that active social involvement, particularly in the community, is the concern of the fellowship. This covers a very wide area of work for which provision should be planned and made.

17. To know that any secular work or activities being followed by members is valued, respected and supported so that people are encouraged to meet non-Christians and play a full and varied part in the community as a whole.

18. To know that there is a positive part for every member to play which has been planned and encouraged.

GOAL SETTING

How trite it is to say 'practise what you preach' and yet how difficult it is to do just that. How can the faith of the church be put into action? Positive goals must be set.

For example, is it possible for us to pray and, in faith, work towards the goal that in the matter of Bible teaching all the main points of Christian doctrine will be covered at every level within 3–5 years? This would be achieved by systematic Bible teaching, inductive and deductive, both from the pulpit and within Bible study groups.

Within a number of years, we would like to see a set number of nurture groups being used on a regular basis and perhaps more Bible study groups ranging from the home-study groups we already have to a deeper study 'school' for those who wish it. Can we not make firm plans for a post-Alpha group to be started and those contacted through it to be fed into home or church-based groups?

Should we not expect that the church will plan a series of activities for couples and families within a 3- or 5-year period, including marriage enrichment courses?

Should not an opportunity be given to every church member, say every three years, to attend a course on how to give away their faith? Each year there should be four in-house evangelistic 'drives' and every two years the church should join in or organise a county- or nation-wide evangelistic outreach.

Can we not, in faith, trust that the fellowship will send out at least five people on short- or long-term missionary work within the coming five years? Can we not write down the percentage figure by which the church will increase its support for full-time workers within the coming three years?

Can we not be flexible enough to plan at least three activities per year in conjunction with other churches or fellowships in our area. And what about our responsibility towards churches overseas? What steps should be taken to arrange church links and visits to our friends in France, Romania and Japan or even Papua New Guinea?

These are some of the things we are thinking about for the future. Many may not be immediately attainable, but it is essential that the fellowship takes a proactive stance and sets specific goals.

Aims

In conclusion, our basic aims as a church may be summarised as follows:

- Unity of the fellowship

- Provision of thorough Bible teaching at all levels

- New Testament-style leadership

- Establishment of a good prayer base

- Evangelism

- Mobilising the membership

- Efficient and practical missionary policy

7

Northwood Hills Evangelical Church, Middlesex

Roger Pearce

Roger came to faith through an SU beach mission at the place where he grew up in Cornwall. After some school-teaching and then training at All Nations, he served in Zambia with SU for ten years. After three years as SU coordinator in south-east England, he was invited to go to Northwood Hills Evangelical Church in 1980 as their first full-time elder, and is still there.

Northwood Hills developed around a new underground station. It was a 1930's growth point in 'Metroland', made romantic but also gently mocked by John Betjeman for its privet-bordered gentility. Situated on the north-west of London, it enjoys excellent commuter connections to the City and the West End where many local people travel to work.

The period saw many faithful initiatives by the 'Brethren' in new urban developments. Prosperous, although modest, meeting halls multiplied across the suburbs, felt to be none the worse for having relatively small congregations. They were tidy ecclesiastical units with pride in their correctness in faith and separated lifestyle. Their members had a warm and vigorous evangelistic vision, a thorough-going knowledge of the word of God, but also a satisfaction with their pattern of worship and church order which may not have anticipated how much change would be needed to keep their evangelism and church life relevant.

INITIAL GROWTH

Windsor Hall was named after the cul-de-sac where it eventually put down roots. The fellowship branched out from a nearby

'Brethren' assembly in the late 1940s and first met in a home. Soon the members hired a hall on Sundays, and then acquired a site just off the shopping parade where they put up a temporary building. The fellowship became established and, in 1961, built a pleasant contemporary building with the help of the Laing Trust. A less permanent all-purpose hall was added behind it on our limited narrow site.

The 1960s brought a period of growth for most churches in this suburban belt – before prosperous Christians moved further out into the green belt in the 1970s – and the church thrived as a moderate-sized forward-looking fellowship. A strongly led youth work brought young people to faith, although there was concern when they often ended up in the large evangelical Anglican church not far away! Each year, the most lively event was a children's mission, usually led by David Lewis, the colourful Scripture Union children's evangelist, whose wife came from a Windsor Hall family. Members of the church were significantly active in interdenominational activities such as the Billy Graham crusades, the North Africa Mission, Scripture Union, and in speaking in other denominational churches.

OPENNESS TO CHANGE

In the 1970s, although encouraging numbers and a good family spirit persisted, there was a growing awareness that the ability to connect with the local community was limited and that the leaders were less able to cope with the pastoral demands. But change was not frowned on, and much thought was given to rethinking methods and structure. Back in the mid 1960s, the name 'Windsor Hall' had been changed to 'Northwood Hills Evangelical Church', since the elders had felt that a continuing identification with 'Brethren', now linked in the eyes of the public with strange 'Exclusive' practices, was becoming a hindrance to effective communication.

There was a steady growth in confidence in viewing things more objectively and biblically. All members of the church family were encouraged to use their gifts. The elders realised the folly of monopolising the whole gamut of spiritual and practical responsibilities and set up a deacons' group chosen by the members. Annual weekends away at Pilgrim Hall were a great September experience of re-grouping after the summer break and of fellowship-strengthening from the mid-1970s through to the late 1980s.

A Full-time Elder

These examples of change represent a period of steady adjustment. But, even with these developments, the life of the church seemed to be on a plateau, with some symptoms of decline. The leaders wondered how they were going to sustain effective leadership through increasingly rapid sociological change. Some elders and other members were regular attenders at Swanwick conferences of 'Brethren', and in 1978 the theme 'Where do we go from here?' strengthened the possibility of appointing a full-time worker.

After carefully persuading the members of the soundness of such thinking, and answering objections without meeting serious opposition, a search was begun. In 1980 a former SU worker, Roger Pearce with his wife Frances, after experience in Scripture Union ministries in Africa and the UK, was invited to come to serve as a full-time elder with authority to give the major continuity in the teaching ministry and to lead the church in pastoral care.

Church Family Service

A desire for a greater pace of development in the church's life had built up and the new full-time elder received warm support in giving a lead. The most marked area of change was in the Sunday programme. Traditional arrangements for a mid-morning breaking of bread and an evening teaching service gave a structure which, however sound, did not unite the potential church family or give a framework for welcoming newcomers.

The main emphasis was now put on a service for the whole fellowship – a teaching service with care to involve all generations, carefully balancing contemporary and traditional materials and communication. Over the next two years, regular numbers increased markedly and, each Sunday, two duplicate services were arranged. To avoid a church with separate sections we hired a nearby school hall once a month so that all could meet together. This 'church family' service, although continually changing in content, has remained similar in spirit and principle since and continues to be the church's main meeting point.

COMMUNION

The vital renewing experience of breaking bread and drinking wine was no longer reserved for a particular time slot. We tried various approaches before we developed a pattern which enables all to have a regular opportunity to participate. Eventually, we developed the principle of holding it at different times on different Sundays; once a month at an early time, once at the main morning service, once in the evening when it is now the conclusion to a fellowship meal. Home groups also have communion as part of their programme. In such ways we tried to work towards these neighbourhood groups being embryonic new churches. We should like to see this make more progress.

HOME GROUPS

Home-based groups had been attempted in the late 1970s. The commitment to them had not been sufficient and they soon died out. When a new attempt to introduce them was made in 1981 there was an initial reluctance to try something that had failed. Therefore, in the new initiative it was emphasised that groups should first learn to enjoy being together, and that they would not be simply times for study and prayer, however vital these elements are, but also places for shared lives and pastoral care structures.

Groups rapidly became established and were considered an essential part of our members' participation in the body. Older members who could not come at night were included in social events and outings. Later, we scrambled all the groups and reconstituted them as local area fellowships, encouraged to arrange social occasions with friends and neighbours included. Although some have been effective in this, it has not proved easy to make it as strong a feature of group life as we would wish. For several years, the groups were strengthened by special support being given to group leaders, with a fortnightly gathering of leaders for training, sharing news, and preparing study and activity materials. Leaders were also helped with an annual progress review.

YOUTH WORKERS

As young families in the church increased, there followed greater demands and opportunities in youth and children's work. Donald Campbell, during his degree studies at London Bible College, shared in the teenage work. In 1986 we had decided to seek a full-time youth worker, and he responded to our invitation. With his gifts for communication he spent four years strengthening our teenage group, leading our holiday club for primary children, and opening up links with schools.

Next, from Moorlands College came Malcolm Reddaway, with his wife Jane. He gave our youth programme an energetic edge, including such features as well-organised and sporty weekend house-parties, and he made good use of modern communication techniques. He was responsible for 'Cross-talk' (see below).

Jonathan and Angela Sharples came to faith through the church and Jonathan later went on to study at LBC. For his apprenticeship, we asked him to serve as assistant minister and youth worker. He specialised in monthly 'cringe-free' special events for adults called 'First Friday', wrote and directed the young people in a Good Friday musical, and wrote songs and performed at holiday clubs with extraordinary inventiveness.

These three moved on to serve at Sutton Coldfield Baptist Church (youth minister), at Rhiwbina Baptist Church (youth minister) and at Springbank Evangelical Church in Campbeltown (full-time worker) respectively. Now, another ex-LBC student, Jonathan Brooks-Martin, with his wife Ruth, has joined us to continue this dimension of our church life.

OTHER HELPERS

Gilbert Kirby, former general secretary of the Evangelical Alliance and principal of LBC, 'retired' among us and provided experience and encouragement. In 1990 Sandra Michie, who had served as a missionary nurse at Lukolwe in Zambia for 25 years, building up a large rural health centre, came to live in Northwood. She quickly began to carry a large share of the pastoral care and now works as a general practice nurse for part of the week and as a pastoral carer in the community on the church's behalf for the rest. We have seen the great benefit of bringing medical expertise, as well as Sandra's practical wisdom, to pastoral support.

NEW PREMISES

The elders had long wanted to expand the church's buildings, but no scheme proved realistic. In 1984 an adjoining piece of land became available, larger than the property already owned, and at right angles to the present buildings, giving an L-shaped area. It was bought and prayed over in faith. Various schemes were considered, but the site proved too difficult a shape and too expensive to develop.

A major move was made in 1987 to hire a local school for our Sunday morning programme. In addition to the service in the hall, we used classrooms for prayer and children's activities, and the dining area for socialising. Though expensive in rent, the four years spent there gave the church a more marked community feel, and our activities were more open and accessible to local people.

Investigations about using the site continued, and it became clear that we needed to enlarge the ground available. We gradually acquired portions of gardens backing on to our property. This was achieved by buying several of the properties for a time, using them for a while as housing for our youth worker, renting to church members or, in one case, providing a refuge for a family in exile. Each time, before reselling, we shortened the garden! Eventually we reshaped our land into a triangle! A Christian architect, with experience of dual development of sites, designed a development comprising a new building for the church's use, and 21 sheltered flats whose sale met the main capital costs of the development. The flats were available in 1992 and the new facilities for the church family were tested with a wedding in December that year!

CONTINUOUS GROWTH

After an initial period of increased interest in the church's life, the years from 1980 saw steady growth but with a constantly changing membership since the local population is relatively mobile. Today, growth is probably inhibited by the far greater demand for pastoral caring and counselling. This arises partly from a troubled society, programmed to seek this kind of help, and partly from our being in touch with more people without a Christian background whose lives have more complicated fault lines. Two hundred or so meet on Sunday mornings and the membership is about 190 adults and 100 children.

These are some of the bare facts. What then of the motivation and the principles of church life? Although the main change pinpointed above was the Sunday service programme, we have in fact worked hard at changing the whole climate of church life. We have tried to take notice of the repeated characteristics of renewal in church life down the centuries and have given deliberate attention to cultivating the historical marks of a healthy church.

THE BUILDING

Buildings are both the blessing and the curse of church life. While the church has to meet somewhere, it seems a key principle that we should not place any limitation on where we meet. When we set out our specifications for a new building, we emphasised its main characteristic as adaptability for varied use, and added that anything which made it suitable for worship would be a bonus. We wanted it to look like a contemporary community building – attractive but neutral – not with a design which, historically and culturally, has been associated with 'church'. We knew that the majority of the population do not choose to go into church buildings, and we felt that we should not require this of them before they were given a chance to observe Christian behaviour and hear an explanation of faith.

The building that resulted is sometimes mistaken for Tesco's and we feel we have succeeded! Our aim was to have a common meeting place for Christians and people from our community. We hoped to escape from the usual image of church buildings being deserted and unwelcoming for most of the week. We would have it open all the time and encourage local people to be there.

We opened the new building at the end of 1992, stressing that 'the church' remains 'the members of the fellowship' – wherever they meet – and that the building should never be referred to as 'the church', since this would be a most unbiblical idea! In other words, we would never 'consecrate' the building in the language of ecclesiastical liturgy. When walls, furniture, or a particular part of a building are considered more holy than other places or things, then these become more important than people. Arguments about equipment, seating, decoration, and expenditure on a building then take on a significance they should never have; they distort the church's agenda and damage relationships between leaders and teams in church life.

Unity in Diversity

At an earlier stage, when we were compelled to hold two services on a Sunday morning, we realised the potential damage from letting people drift into different preferences, thus losing the integrity of church life. This was the first prompt to use a school hall to keep our fellowship together. We have planned our whole programme recognising that Christians should not escape the obligation to live together in a community containing differences. That is the negative way to put it.

A more positive way is to say that we need to teach our fellowships that the Spirit of God gives different gifts which are only exercised healthily when Christians respect, accept, and honour each other. We expect our services over a period to have real variety. This variety may be in music, songs and hymns, or modes of worship. We have worked hard to avoid becoming a church with a particular flavour. We teach that Christians need to grow in accepting one another and feel that Romans 15:5–7 gives us a vital dynamic for fellowship life:

> May the God who gives endurance and encouragement give you a spirit of unity among yourselves as you follow Christ Jesus, so that with one heart and mouth you may glorify the God and Father of our Lord Jesus Christ. Accept one another, then, just as Christ accepted you, in order to bring praise to God.

Fellowship Life

To the same end we feel that we have to recognise that our inherited tradition of worship, so dominated by the pious ambience of a

Sunday service in tidy rows, is not a good reproduction of the atmosphere described in the New Testament church. Worship may be considered to be the key factor in church life but, when offered in an absence of loving and serving relationships between Christians, it can so easily be a mockery of the agenda the Lord himself has given us. He modelled washing feet as a key principle and attacked tidy but insincere worship which does not issue in real-life humble service. When the apostles applied their theology, they continually stressed relationships in church life using many words qualified by 'together' and those which describe attitudes and actions towards 'each other'. Linked with the latter are *forgiving, accepting, loving, agreeing with, caring for, encouraging, building up, offering hospitality to, living in harmony with* ... each other.

So we have encouraged the use of every opportunity to build social relationships in fellowship life as the context of our worshipping, teaching and praying. We realise that Christians need to examine themselves in the spirit of 1 Corinthians 11 where the lack of genuine fellowship, sharing, and equality between Christians meant that the taking of bread and wine was without true meaning however correct the words and sentiments expressed. Therefore, although house-based fellowship groups are encouraged to make the study of the word and prayer central to their agenda, the members are also urged to have a real social life together, growing continually in their commitment to each other. We would expect friendships to develop which would leave no one who is ill without visitors, and no one having a baby without meals frequently provided by others during recovery. Of course, we don't always succeed!

No Unnecessary Cultural Oddity

It seems a key aspect of the flexible community-related fellowship modelled in Acts that the social barriers between church and society were not heightened by cultural oddity. There was undoubtedly a moral difference, or holiness, which marked people off, but in history we have allowed this to become far too strong a cultural barrier. We live in ecclesiastical ghettos and are defensive and unnecessarily separatist if we seek to follow one who expected us to be 'in the world but not of it'. A policeman being baptised recently said that the key conversations which led him to commitment were between the players in the church football team. A Chinese lady baptised on the same day cited the keep fit group as her way of 'getting into the church'!

OPENNESS IN FELLOWSHIP

Another fresh discovery of the New Testament model, however obvious, is openness in fellowship. While evangelical Christians tend to be able to define salvation through grace, very few seem to transfer this thinking to relationships so that these in turn are based on grace! And because so many Christians try to earn their salvation, even after conversion, using the world's way of measuring success by comparing oneself with others, service ministries in church life are often pursued competitively. When mixed with a love of gossip, designed to put others down, we have a potent dynamic leading to division, either with groups splitting off and starting new churches, or in painful disagreement and party spirit within a fellowship.

So, in every part of church life, we try to work at learning relationships of grace and forgiveness. When Roger Forster spoke to a gathering of our church leaders in the 1980s he stressed that any Christian church needs to have a leadership group which enjoys and models loving, trusting, humble, and supportive relationships. We have attempted to avoid the frequent limitation in evangelical churches which results in elders and other influential members not being required to submit to the scriptural requirements that Christians are to respect, honour, and love one another!

SHARING OF RESPONSIBILITIES AND GIFTS

A further aspect of this is in the sharing of responsibilities and gifts between men and women. While elders continue to carry the particular responsibility of taking decisions there is a resolve to involve all church members in consultation. We have tried to move away from eldership practised as though the key things happen when the 'board of directors' meets. Through gatherings of home group leaders, consultations with leaders from all activities, specific leaders invited to elders' meetings, and regular prayer, planning and social occasions for elders and wives, we attempt to knit the whole church family together.

CHURCH IDENTITY

What is our church identity? We began with a strong consciousness of being in the 'Brethren' movement. This sense of belonging was unquestioned for thirty years of the church's life. Then followed the period of realising that the unfortunate publicity from the more 'closed' varieties of the 'Brethren' adversely affected our public image. This was partly countered by the good name of the church, gained chiefly through the annual children's activity.

Another move was to stop calling the building a 'hall', and to widen the church's local identity from the street in which it was located to the whole community. We changed our name from 'Windsor Hall' to 'Northwood Hills Evangelical Church'.

Our attitude to the building has now changed, as described above, and today we have chosen a neutral, easy-to-use name for our location. When we bought our extra land there was a derelict house on it, which volunteers pulled down on Saturdays to make way for the present development. We retained its name, 'Fairfield', so as to remove as far as possible the stigma many people associate with official 'church' buildings and which gives them a resolve not to be seen dead (or until dead!) in one!

However, alongside concern about the public image were the potential internal stresses of escaping from the authoritative ecclesiastical traditions that handicapped the 'Brethren'. In numerous churches, so many assumptions had grown up about the right way to do things that a person's soundness was in question if these traditions were queried, defined, or brought into the light of scriptural principles. The appeal to an unidentified authority (although usually attributed to 'the Lord') was expressed by the upholder of 'Brethren' ways in a manner which expected no dissent! And, as a result, many people in such fellowships were deprived of the opportunity and spur to think biblically.

The leaders at Windsor Hall had never been handicapped by such shibboleths and, while they were not radical reformers, they had been realistic in applying a biblical spirit to new challenges.

Change had been gently and pastorally worked through, while safe-guarding the trust of the fellowship at each step. A sense of obligation to remain in contact and in working relationship with other 'Brethren' assemblies became less. The weary, never-ending debate over the apparent sacredness of certain procedures or practices was unattractive, if only because it hindered the development of new opportunities for church-building and neighbourhood witness.

In the 1970s and '80s a stronger independence of spirit evolved. This revealed itself in a sense of freedom in deliberately thinking through all areas of church services, leadership patterns, and fellowship groups in the light of scripture and not tradition. Partnerships with other local denominations in sharing arrangements for home-based fellowship groups and joint youth events replaced links with nearby 'Brethren' assemblies.

Ironically it was the coming of a full-time elder that brought some restoration of contact with these assemblies who, by this time, had made their own more independent moves. Now, through personal relationships between leaders, and the participation of full-time workers, there is a different and more promising link, with encouragement from Partnership. This has yet to win a similar level of interest in church members.

LINKS WITH OTHER CHURCHES

Alternative new links with other local churches come and go, but are part of the more flexible style which now characterises the church's agenda. For some years, mainly under our church's leadership, there were extensive arrangements for inter-church home-based fellowship groups for short periods, mainly in Lent. We helped to mobilise over 400 local church members in over 30 groups, and to give training, study outlines and support to leaders. At another time, after a joint local evangelistic fortnight shared by the churches, a regular joint youth event, 'Crosstalk', was arranged at Fairfield for several local churches as a follow-on activity.

Such initiatives, taking up shorter-term opportunities, are now a key feature of church life. There is a readiness to try a new approach; and if it does not bear fruit it can be dropped. We feel it important to escape the former official attitude which hesitated to start something new because we needed to be sure it would endure as a structure. The essence of the New Testament church seemed to be flexibility, with the result that the church remained relevant – while retaining its unchanging truth. We feel that any structures can be changed; the key issues are not structures but relationships in Christ and the relevance of the word to both Christians and outsiders.

TIDDLYWINKS

Experimentation has therefore become a theme of church development. And, if a new venture is begun, we go at it as thoroughly as possible. One such was a parent and pre-school children session – 'Tiddlywinks' – begun in earnest in the early 1980s. Before starting, several members went to an evening class to train for such a venture, and careful thought was given to equipment and to the whole philosophy of the activity. It would be an act of service for the younger families in our local community with no overt evangelism. It would provide a meeting place between Christians and others, where friendships could develop. Patience in establishing relationships would be exercised with a trust that the Lord would open people's hearts to his kindness through the team, and prompt questions about our faith.

This quickly became an effective and popular ministry which was recommended to families by local health staff. For many years, there have been church teams operating on three different days with attendances of over 300 parents and children each week. This has given us a network of contacts in the community and has been the most fruitful area of friendship evangelism and, consequently, new Christians becoming members.

MINISTERING TO MEN

Over time, the need to focus on men became significant, since most – but not all – of the parents who come to the daytime activities are women. One approach, pursued for three years, was evening classes with subjects chosen with men mainly in mind: golf lessons; classes in computer skills, decorating, photography. Out of these came new relationships and the strengthening of ones already forming. Another development was the formation of a home group which

came to specialise in linking older people on the fringe of the fellowship. Several of these have made commitments since.

The most effective recent meeting place has been through football. One of our full-time youth workers recruited a team which
joined a local league. It continues to be a very helpful life-sharing
structure, leading to faith-discovering. It has been particularly helpful in enabling husbands of wives who have become Christians to
have an easier way into church life and hearing the Christian message. It provides a more helpful route than being required to come
and sit in a Sunday service, something which is often too big a
cultural step for a male without any previous Christian input. Table
quiz evenings and a pantomime have also been a draw for the
community.

A COMMUNITY CENTRE

We have aimed, in outreach, not to put all our eggs in any one basket
but to adopt a total approach that builds relationships with people
in the community as spontaneously as possible. In the same spirit,
we have made our building into a community centre. It is open
through the week by having a job-sharing office team to welcome
all-comers. There is a full programme with parent and toddler activity, keep fit groups, and an open-house coffee shop filling most of
the time-slots from Monday to Friday. All these are run by church
members.

The building is made available to local community groups,
including the residents' association, the bowling club, the allot-
ments society, and many others. Groups from organisations like the
Cottage Hospital come for fund-raising events. We continually have
to make judgments about the limits of such openness, in regard to
the ethos and aims of different groups. However, when we grow in
our ability to share our lives within the Christian fellowship, our
social relationships make it easier for us to include others who are
outside a faith position. Fears of gospel issues being compromised
do not materialise. It means that, when relationships have been built
up, there is an opportunity for people to hear the gospel, not as an
unfamiliar shock, but in a context of trust in which the truths can be
observed in Christian character and attitude as well as in word.

Community-related activities have been prompted by church

members' links. Since 1995, we have invited people with learning difficulties to Fairfield on Sunday afternoon every few weeks. Large numbers of disabled friends and their carers now join us for singing, drama, story-telling and tea.

Another recent emphasis has been on preparing our young people for leaving home. We have seen the opportunity of short-term voluntary service schemes, and have supported young people who have served with Careforce, the Africa Inland Mission in Kenya, and Latin Link STEP teams in Latin America.

WORLD MISSION

London Bible College is a near neighbour, and we acknowledge the stimulus from this link. Our main connections come through students who settle into the community and opt for participation in our fellowship life. Their high motivation is a gift to the church. Their eagerness to take on responsibilities, often as practical parts of their curriculum, provides extra hands, fresh vigour and ideas.

This, in turn, has affected our mission links with the wider world. Some students have remained part of the church's life after they have left college and have eventually gone overseas in missionary service. The ongoing support we give to them, and to others from our fellowship who have gone abroad, has given us extensive and strong personal links with other parts of the world. Last Christmas Day we had live phone link-ups into our service with those we support in the Philippines, Argentina, and India.

A missionary society we support has found our facilities ideal for interviews, staff training times, Saturday supporters' events, and volunteer orientation weekends. This has helped our membership to become more aware of sharing faith across cultures.

ALPHA

The Alpha evangelistic programme has provided a welcome new impetus. Two years ago we organised our first video course. We invited church members, as well as those outside of Christian faith, to participate. The purpose was not only to give them a training experience for their own benefit but also to gain confidence in it and stimulate them to invite friends to later courses. About 80 met for a meal every Wednesday evening.

This has led to a continuous mid-week evening 'food + faith' programme all through the year. We usually run an Alpha course, but also provide other options to chose from. We have groups for people who have completed Alpha and are either still asking similar questions ('Know More') or want to consider commitment ('On the Edge') and, sometimes, for members who want to strengthen Christian faith and knowledge ('Grow More'). The openness, warm relationships, and frankness possible in this format is attractive and has been another aid in breaking down the uncomfortable cultural barriers which prevent Christians and non-Christians from being in communication.

CONCLUSION

The development of the church has resulted not only from conscious themes and goals in the leaders' minds but also from all the disturbing pressures, missed opportunities, and untidiness which are an inevitable part of the local church and community scene. Our leaders may well have been thought over-hesitant in forwarding radical measures – particularly in contemporary worship, faith and the charismatic issue – which many see as vital in making the Christian cause more effective in our culture.

The emphasis at Fairfield has been strongly on ecclesiology, the structure and dynamics of church life, on distinguishing between what is traditional and what is cultural, and on more spontaneous church-building which issues from scriptural principles. There has been a determination to win a freedom to be biblical which, contrary to many expectations, leads not to limitation and narrowness, but to flexibility, a positive opportunism and relevance. Our priority has been the quality of our fellowship. There has been a strong desire to avoid the suspicion and misunderstanding so often associated with change. We have worked to foster trust, humility of spirit, and flexible thinking. While aiming to give a firm lead in shaping church programmes, we have sought to put greater emphasis on the context – such as attitudes, responsibilibity to sustain loving relationships, openness to members' feelings – rather than on the leadership decision itself. The key factor is trust.

8

Southview Evangelical Church, Chirnside, Scotland

Ken Brown

Norma and Ken grew up in the central belt of Scotland where they were grounded in typical 'Brethren' churches. Study at Northumbria Bible College, where Ken gained the external London BD degree, opened their eyes to a wider Christian perspective. While students, they entered fully into the life of Southview Evangelical Church, Chirnside and, after graduation six years ago, they were invited to stay on in a full-time capacity.

Occupying a strategic position overlooking the rich farmlands of Eastern Berwickshire, Chirnside is approximately seven miles from the historic town of Berwick-upon-Tweed, and the same distance from Duns, the county town. For many years the village has functioned as an agricultural service centre, catering for the needs of the large arable farms surrounding it and also for those who live within the farming community.

In recent years, with the onset of mechanisation, many farms have been working with only a tiny percentage of their previous staff levels. A number of light industries, including fish and potato processing, grain storage and distribution, have formed as offshoots from the traditional ones. The main employer for many years, however, has been the America-based Dexter Corporation who run a large paper-processing mill just south of the village. Largely owing to this, the population of Chirnside, unlike the Border area in general, increased by nearly forty per cent between 1971 and 1981. It now remains steady at around 1200, with another few hundred occupying the surrounding countryside. This type of employment presents particular problems. There is a large amount of shift working, and wage levels are among the lowest in the whole of Scotland.

The growth of a large local authority housing area in the seventies to cope with the mill development dramatically changed the physical appearance of the village. These houses, in the main, were occupied by a host of incoming workers from places as far afield as Glasgow and Newcastle, which gives the village, twenty years on, a distinctly cosmopolitan feel. This is unlike the predominant parochial nature of the Borders community in general. This factor has undoubtedly been crucial in the growth of the church in recent years in an area where the wider church picture is bleak.

Nearly 200 children attend the village primary school which includes two nursery classes and a special needs unit. Children of secondary school age travel to Duns. A major negative for the area, is the lack of good quality further education facilities. This means that we invariably lose whole generations of young people to the large conurbations, very few of whom ever return.

CLAIMS TO FAME

Two men of world repute knew Chirnside as home. David Hume, the renowned moral philosopher, went to school in Chirnside until he was twelve, before going on to study law. His family home was Ninewells Estate, now owned by one of Southview's elders. It is ironic that in the birthplace of one of the world's greatest religious thinkers a small group of Christians are seeking daily to undermine his enormous influence.

Jim Clark, world motor racing champion, lived and farmed at Chirnside. Tragically killed at the Hockenheim circuit at the age of twenty-nine, he is the inspiration for many of our local youth. Hundreds of people come to Chirnside each year to pay tribute at his grave in the local churchyard, and to photograph his memorial in the centre of the village. Local people still remember the day when the whole village turned up to welcome him home after his world championship victory. Such moments don't happen often in the life of an otherwise anonymous village.

CHRISTIAN HERITAGE

Chirnside's Christian heritage is strong. In the 1860s there were three parish churches in Chirnside alone, the earliest tracing its origins back to the twelfth century. In addition, a number of mission halls functioned over the years, but all have closed. A measure of the decline in the established church is seen in the number of ministers serving the county. From over twenty in 1969, the number has slumped to ten, and there is pressure for further reduction. Some Church of Scotland ministers now look after up to five separate parishes. This state of affairs would sadden the 'greats' of past years, especially those who suffered in covenanting times.

The following inscription can be found in Chirnside Church:

In memory of Reverend Henry Erskine sometime minister of this Parish, who was eminently distinguished by his incorruptible integrity in private life, undaunted zeal in the service of his heavenly Master and steady attachment to the religious principles of the Church of Scotland at a time when the profession of these principles often led to imprisonment and exile, both of which he endured with exemplary resignation and fortitude.

Erskine died in 1696, but it is difficult to get away from his example, especially when the street you live in is named in his memory!

SOUTHVIEW IN THE PAST

The history of Southview may not be so colourful but in many ways it is just as inspiring. Chirnside is one of those interesting examples of a 'Brethren' church formed independently of contact with the movement elsewhere. The Revival magazine referred in 1865 to a 'good work being done in Chirnside' and it appears that, a few years later, the church aligned itself with the Brethren movement as a whole. Over the hundred or so years that followed it was never numerically strong although, because its membership included some prominent members of the business community, it always seemed to box above its weight. The second world war took its toll, with a number of the next generation not returning, and the church seemed at that stage to be in terminal decline.

By 1960 only five women remained. The situation, humanly speaking, was desperate. They would break bread if a man joined them – and many did, coming from as far afield as Newcastle and Edinburgh, a return trip of 120 miles. The only regular activities were prayer, and the ever present children's work. The church became known as 'The Mission', taking on the label of the mission halls which had all now gone. By 1970 there had been a small recovery with a few people moving into the area but, as recently as 1990, membership was still in the low twenties.

DRAMATIC TURNAROUND

Today, however, the situation is dramatically different. The church has a membership of approaching 70 people. Sunday services frequently attract congregations of up to 100. Sunday school and Bible class, defunct for many years, now thrive again. The church is led by a pastor, and also employs a community worker. The finance necessary for this was unthinkable only a few years ago.

A CHURCH FOR THE COMMUNITY

By the summer of 1998 a new building programme, costing in the region of £120,000, had been completed, giving facilities for a seven-day-a-week service to a community which the previous building could not deliver. The new facilities allow the establishment of a community project including a coffee room, an information service in conjunction with the existing Health and Social Care agencies, a village visitation programme, a 'drop-in' facility for youth, and much more. The scope for further development is considerable.

These developments will build on a strong base of contact within our village, built up over a number of years, particularly with children and the elderly. Our existing mid-week programme includes various groups for children and youth, attended by up to 100, supplemented in the summer by two holiday clubs. Regular coffee mornings are held for the senior members of our community. Younger adults are not forgotten, since events such as supper evenings, dinners, concerts and barbecues are held with relational and evangelistic emphases. Members of the church are now regularly involved in our community through bodies such as parent/teacher associations, school boards, tenants' committees, and so on, and the church plays a full part in events such as the annual gala week.

Early on in the planning process for the building development programme, I was reminded of the goal of the project by a retired Methodist minister, who has become a great friend of our congregation. He said, 'Do you want to continue as an overgrown mission hall, or do you want to step out with the goal of being a fully integrated church in a needy community?' In all our planning, the latter goal has underpinned our thinking.

As part of my visitation responsibilities I visit an elderly man in his nineties. He was a member of Southview in the early 1950s when closure seemed the most likely scenario. His question is quite simple. 'How has such a turn around been possible?' I am confronted with the same question as I write this account.

WHY THE TURN AROUND?

I didn't find this question easy to answer then, and I still don't. Church growth seems to me to be essentially a work of God. Where is the rational explanation for a church consisting of a small number of people, some thirty years later, thriving and continuing to grow? Humanly speaking, there is no explanation. What follows, therefore, is not an ABC of church growth principles but some simple reflections on the past few years in our church. It is an intensely personal and practical response to the moving of God's Spirit in a rural environment where, especially in recent years, decline has been seen as inevitable.

GOD HAS NOT CHANGED

I have decided to divide the remainder of this account into two. First, the focus will be on the spiritual aspect of what has happened; then the focus will change to the practical, commonsense side of church life. In practice the two are not separate, but it aids our understanding to make such a division.

Chirnside began as a result of revival in the mid-nineteenth century. A very simple principle follows which many, I suspect, have since forgotten: God has not changed.

It is my belief that the idea that we live in a day of small things has been a crippling factor leading to disaster for churches such as our own. Not only is it based on poor theology; it is the easiest way known to modern man of relieving ourselves of responsibility. If we believe that God isn't going to do anything then, in practice, we have every excuse to sit back and let him get on with doing nothing! The result is an awful waste of natural and supernatural resources, many of which we must have spurned over the years. A church leadership – for that is inevitably where it must begin – that has no expectation of seeing growth has surely failed properly to understand God's desire to work new things in our individual and collective lives, as one generation succeeds another.

A biblical principle which has been very pertinent to Chirnside in recent years is summed up in the phrase: 'just at the right time.' The idea is that all things come together so that the will of God can be worked out. It is an impossibility for men and women to have any input into this divine timetable or to have any understanding of the thinking behind it. Many times over the eight years or so that I have attended this church I have been very conscious of times and events that are, according to human logic, inexplicable. As a church we have therefore been overwhelmed with supernatural coincidences.

PROVISION OF FULL-TIME WORKERS

For example, just when the small church was striving to move on from its traditional 'Brethren' past, along came a couple who were going through Bible college in the locality with a similar background and outlook. They had a desire to move on with God while retaining the best of their church heritage, though they were unsure of the plausibility of this since doubts had grown in their minds over a number of years as a result of their experience of seeing legalism run rampant in Scottish 'Brethren' circles. God's timing was perfect and at the end of their four years of training, Southview had employed their first full-time workers. Quite an achievement for a church of barely thirty members!

UNITED CHRISTIAN WITNESS IN THE VILLAGE

Within two months of this significant event, another major step forward was to occur. For twenty years or so there had been no meaningful contact with the Church of Scotland in the village. The then minister had been *in situ* for the whole of that period and he was not favourably disposed towards independent congregations. In short, there was a major problem, in that the Christian witness was divided and was seen to be so by the local population. However, the picture changed almost overnight when the incumbent decided to move and a new parish minister was appointed, one with whom co-operation and joint encouragement and development was easier to engender. For the past four years there have been joint services during Lent and Easter, including pulpit exchanges and, more importantly, growing integration of the respective congregations. This factor has been vital in raising Southview's profile and effectiveness in the community. This past year saw the best manifestation yet of this new found fellowship when, together, we hosted an Alpha course with up to forty people attending, with the result that many people experienced significant spiritual development. Undoubtedly, God has been at work in this whole process.

IMPROVED FACILITIES

God's timing has also been evident in the practical development of our facilities. For years we had been restricted by buildings which, although meeting the vision of their day, were now too small and increasingly inflexible. Their great asset was that they were right in the heart of the village. Their greatest drawback was that this position limited development, since the church owned no ground around the site.

In the summer of 1996, when the need was being felt most acutely, an adjoining property consisting of two retail premises came on to the market. Within weeks the deals were done, and God had shown once again that his timing was perfect. It has taken nearly two years to plan and build, a period which I confess has felt frustratingly long at times but, again, the divine angle has been evident in that as a church we have needed time to reflect on the possibility of social and community involvement, a difficult concept for many. However, now that principle is unanimously accepted.

Community Involvement

So we go forward into a new era together. Part of this process, again timely, is involvement in a pilot scheme within the UK action arm of Tearfund. Twenty-five churches from different theological, geographical and social backgrounds were invited to participate during 1998 in a programme of training with a view to putting community action on a solid footing within the church. We feel privileged to be asked to be part of the process and have relished the experience.

One of the greatest strengths of Southview is also one of its greatest weaknesses. Owing to the rural nature of Berwickshire, church members live in over a dozen different communities across the county. This is strategically important now, and will be increasingly so in the future, as a Christian presence is maintained in small villages with struggling parish churches. Out of thirty or so Church of Scotland congregations that cover the area, more than half are in danger of closing in the next ten years. If these do finally disappear whole communities will be without a Christian witness. So, committed Christians who use Southview as a base while seeking to serve in their own villages are engaged in an exciting and pioneering work. However, this geographical spread of membership causes difficulties. Historically, Southview's base of Chirnside has not been well served by a daily Christian presence.

When we began our ministry five years ago, only one (elderly) church member lived in the village apart from ourselves, and within two weeks we were participating in her funeral service. The position looked bleak but, against the worrying background of rural de-population, God steadily but surely brought new Christians into the village. Now there is a strong representation with a number of new converts. There is no explanation for this other than the timing of God and his apparent will to revitalise the Christian community in an altogether insignificant village.

Please don't ask me to explain the reasons for this. I simply do not know and I doubt if I ever shall. But I firmly believe, because of the experiences we have known, that God has a plan for our community, and his actions over the past five to ten years bear this out.

A man for whom I have tremendous respect, who is now well on in years and is not prone to wild statements, felt constrained to tell us a few years ago that he felt the words of the Lord to Solomon at the dedication of the Temple, recorded in 2 Chronicles 2 : 7, were appropriate to our situation: 'I have heard your prayer and have chosen this place for myself as a temple for sacrifices.'

At the time, I was reminded immediately of the example of those few women who prayed for blessing and believed that their prayers would be answered. I am in no doubt that God will answer their prayers in a fuller way too, in accordance with his words to Solomon. Answered prayer and living, effective and growing churches are surely close to the heart of God. To be part of such a move of the Spirit is, at the same time, deeply humbling and tremendously exciting. I suspect that is the way it is meant to be.

When I first began working with Southview, I took out a blank sheet of A4 paper, and wrote at the top: 'Steps in church growth' (a step of faith in itself). Over the years it has been encouraging to get that sheet of paper out from time to time and to add little sentences or phrases which have been relevant as the church has changed and grown. As I now go into the practical aspects of the growth that Southview has known, these thoughts are based on those notes taken on a very much *ad hoc* basis over the years. They will be in no particular order and for many other churches they may be irrelevant, but they have been important and necessary for us. So I hope and trust that they may be of help to other people in similar situations.

BUILDING ON EXISTING STRENGTHS

One of the first things we realised we had to do was to build on the existing strengths of the church as it was. The church was small and its resources were limited, but over a number of years the work among the children of the village had been very strong. A recent survey was done by a student working with the church on placement as part of a degree research project. He interviewed and contacted many people in the local community, and discovered that the children's work was the one area that gained most respect within the community. Therefore it was felt to be right that it should be regarded not, as it is so often, as the Cinderella of church life but as the foundation of church life and development.

WORKING WITH CHILDREN

One of the problems we faced, which many others come across today, is that children can stop attending the various activities around the age of nine or ten and become lost to the church. We realised that we had to put a strategy in place for keeping children through all ages. This meant that, instead of the traditional children's meeting which catered for all primary school age children, we had to establish two clubs for that age range and cater for them differently, according to their particular age and background. There had to be something in place that was relevant for children of eleven beginning their secondary education. This need produced the development of a new club.

We have developed new ways of working with children. Our annual holiday club which has been running for over seven years has, on average, over eighty children attending each day. This has enabled us to develop contacts with families and invite them to social events such as barbecues and dinners. We also encourage the children to start the habit of attending church on Sundays, with or without their parents, as well as during the week.

We have also recognised the need to train our leaders to be more effective in the work in which they are involved; to encourage them, to pastor them, and to ensure they are resourced to do the job effectively.

Something that has taken a little longer has been getting the right people into the right jobs. Over the years, our churches have been prone to being run by activists, while many others remain in their homes and let everyone else get on with it. That sometimes works, but on many occasions it doesn't because you end up with square pegs in round holes. So, quietly, we try to encourage people to find out what their niche is, and to harness their willingness, enthusiasm and expertise.

LIVING IN THE COMMUNITY

The second aspect worth mentioning is the firm belief we have that it is important, if not vital, to live within the community in which you seek to minister. Thankfully, God worked a miracle in allowing my wife and me to move into the community when it seemed impossible. This move has been a tremendous plus factor for the congregation, as local people have built up a trust and respect because we have a desire to live, work and socialise with them. This is not always easy as church life can often be time-consuming, but it is important to take time to programme, prioritise, and discipline oneself to spend time with local people. Incarnational ministry – or living with the people – we regard as vitally important. Many opportunities to serve come our way because of it.

This happens in many ways, more in the tragedies than in the joys of local life. In the summer of 1997, just prior to a mission period we were undertaking as a church, we awoke on a Sunday morning to hear of a fatal car accident in the village. The youngsters involved were known to the villagers, and such situations shake a community to its core. That Sunday evening, after the service, I remained around the area of the church and, before long, well over fifteen young people were inside the building. Many of them were crying; others just reflecting on the tragedy which had broken into their lives.

Situations like that are possible only when you live and work with the people. Much of it is simply commonsense: encouraging church members to get involved in parent/teacher associations or school boards; making sure that you are represented at quiz nights for local organisations in the village; being involved in the Gala week of the village once a year when people socialise. One of the highlights in our ministry was in 1996. The local Church of Scotland minister was going to be away at the time of the crowning of the Gala Queen, and we were asked to give the prayer of dedication and thanksgiving. It was a sign of acceptance, one which we had striven for, and which we were delighted to receive.

This process can be helped by taking out time to research and reflect on local church history and culture. Visits to the library can pay off. You discover books and pamphlets which provide wonderful insights into the background of the community of which you were unaware. Talks and conversations with the elderly residents of the community can also be enlightening as you discover past events which still have an impact on the present.

Using External Resources

Another practical principle which we sought to put in place was to make use of external resources when these are available. Very early on, we had to recognise that not all the gifts, ideas and people that we would love to have in our church were necessarily there at any given time. So, over the years, we have built up relationships with Tearfund, with Youth for Christ in our Friday evening Rock Solid club for teenagers, with Scripture Union in training for our children's workers, and with Alpha. Such contacts help to alleviate the parochialism which is a problem needing constant attention in rural settings.

Bible Teaching

Turning to the internals of church life, many changes have taken place over the years. One of the main ones has been the introduction of the consecutive Bible teaching ministry which we have regarded as vitally important in our development as a church congregation. People have been strengthened and spiritually developed in a positive way because of this change.

It never ceases to amaze me that many of our churches which regard themselves as being biblically superior are full of people who have a disastrously low understanding of the content of scripture. We have sought to address this, both doctrinally in people's understanding of scripture, and also pastorally, as people are made aware in a systematic way of the requirements of the Christian life. This thinking has developed in mid-week courses such as 'Bible foundations' and 'Personal witnessing' which look into specific areas to help us increase our knowledge and understanding of the Bible in a practical way.

We are now in a situation where approximately fifty to sixty per cent of the teaching within the church is undertaken by the pastor himself. Part of the teaching process has also been to cultivate an openness to change, making people more aware of the society and culture in which we live. This process has been helped for us at Southview by strong links with Northumbria Bible College, with the steady flow of students giving us freshness and flexibility in our approach.

This has been seen most clearly in the past two years as we have struggled as a congregation with the concept of community and social action. Questions have had to be faced, such as: What is appropriate and what is not? Are we really in danger of embracing a social gospel? What does scripture actually say about these things? Time has been taken to delve into these issues and gain a biblical perspective which is relevant for us in our circumstances.

New Structures

The development of structures within church life has also been vitally important. The appointment of two full-time workers has already been mentioned and has proved to be a great catalyst for progress. The leadership has developed in its structure through the appointment of deacons, and the subsequent decision to move to a leadership team format with various groups looking after different aspects of church life. Equally helpful has been the encouragement of small groups, whether it be for the elderly members of our congregation, for the young mums as they meet to study together, and for the proper and consistent care of new converts – an area which we were very concerned about in past years. Now a new convert in our church will automatically be assigned to a mentor or person they trust and respect, and a relationship will be built up over a number of years as they are integrated into church life. All of these structures have been seen as vital for us in planning for future growth.

Other developments will come as no surprise – such as an enhanced prayer life, less self-focused, more targeted on the community and the people with whom we have contact. We have prayed more intelligently as we better understand the circumstances of life around us. A deepening of the fellowship and the increasing level of pastoral care within the church have become obvious, too, as the years passed. The issues we have had to face at a pastoral level have often taken us to our limits. Included here is the encouraging and practising of the priesthood of all believers – a doctrine much beloved in our circles but very often sadly lacking in practice.

Some months ago, after some particular special event, it was a great encouragement to look around at those involved and to find that a significant proportion of the church had been involved in the planning, preparation, and carrying out of the event. It is hard at Southview to remain in the background, because you are encouraged and, we hope, resourced to carry out specific roles in the church.

WORSHIP AND FELLOWSHIP

Another great blessing that has occurred at Southview over the past five years in particular is that, as these internal church matters have progressed, other areas of our church life, such as worship and fellowship, have moved forward also. We have been encouraged by the numbers of people who in past years would never have considered becoming part of our congregation, joining with us. It is probably true that around half of our membership are now not from a 'Brethren' background. This, as you can imagine, brings bonuses as well as difficulties. Many of our congregation come from Methodist, Pentecostal, Baptist and other traditions, and we feel that they enrich our public and private worship together. This has not been perceived as a threat but as a blessing, and in reality it has turned out to be so.

LINKS WITH OTHER CHURCHES

We have also sought as a fellowship to become much more involved in the wider church scene in our own locality. This has happened over the past five or so years as we have developed relations with the local parish church, and Southview has taken its place in the wider church scene in the Eastern Borders. For many evangelicals who struggle within their own traditional congregations, Southview is seen as a leader and a catalyst for change in this area. The main difficulty has been not so much people in our own congregation struggling with wider church involvement – although that has been the case for some – but rather the reactions from other church leaders who have grown to see Southview and its progress as a threat and a challenge to their own survival.

LINKS WITH SOCIAL AGENCIES

A more recent development, seen as crucial to the success of our community project, has been the establishment of links with many of the social agencies which work in our local community. These include contacts with the social work department, the health services, and the providers of houses for the village. We have been encouraged as agencies such as these have felt free to discuss with us the possibilities of working together to help and empower the people of our local communities. Many of our members work within these agencies and we have been encouraged at the response of their superiors and contemporaries as to the possibilities of working with a local church. This is seen as a crucial area to develop further in the next three to five years.

CONCLUSION

My late father was a great user of alliteration in his sermons. While putting these reflections together, I have been drawn to three words which perhaps encapsulate the vision and practice of Southview:

- *Imagination* – a focus on vision and development;

- *Integration* – a focus on church unity and fellowship; building each other up and caring for each other in a way that stands as a witness to onlookers;

- *Incarnation* – the desire to focus on community involvement, not only talking to the people outside the church but living among them.

So, there it is: the story of how a church born in a nineteenth-century revival has itself, towards the end of the twentieth century, been revived. It is a simple story, and it is true to say that none of the changes recorded above has been too difficult to bring about. For that we are very thankful, and hope and pray that this will be the case with future changes.

We are, however, very much aware that the reviving of a local church does not necessarily mean the effective evangelisation of a local community. There is no doubt that what has happened at Southview over the past few years has, especially in the rural context, been impressive, but we are also very much aware that something approaching eighty- to eighty-five per cent of our local community is completely untouched by what is happening within the four walls of our church building. The increasing secularisation of society means that the polarisation of the church and the community will continue.

It is also true that, for those churches which have abandoned the legalistic traditions of the past, there is a danger that their congregations, as they seek to identify with local communities, become almost indistinguishable from them. The result is churches which are very comfortable, happy and content, but also very short-lived. Increasingly, Christians find it easier to conform to society than to seek to transform society. This is a difficult problem which all of us must struggle with in the future. Much hard work is required to re-establish what a church in a community is really all about. There is no doubt that there is an increasing evangelistic awareness, even in the rural environment. We all have a hard task ahead. Though encouraged, we are not under any illusions that the transformation we have seen brings us to the brink of revival in our community. Much hard work, much hard thinking, much hard prayer remains to be done.

Nevertheless, we can give thanks to God for what he has done, for the way in which he has encouraged a congregation which almost became extinct, and for the way he continues to lead us on in the hope that he will do a new thing with us and through us.

9

Tiverton Christian Fellowship, Selly Oak, Birmingham

David Obrey and John Lanchbury

David is married, with four grown-up children. After working in industry for 32 years he has spent a short while with the Birmingham City Mission and the last three years with Cornerstone (not the building society but a Christian charity which engages in and assists churches involved in community work).

John is an educational psychologist who is married, with two small children.

Both are elders of Tiverton Christian Fellowship.

In the last century, Selly Oak was a small village in the county of Worcester; now it is a suburb of Birmingham, situated three miles south-west of the city centre. Owing to conditions made upon the builders of the Birmingham-Worcester canal by the local landowners, the village was the first location on the canal after leaving Birmingham where wharves could be built. As a consequence, several factories were established, including brass and copper rolling mills and the beginnings of a motor cycle and machine tool industry. George Cadbury developed his chocolate 'factory in a garden', one mile away at what was to be named Bournville. Today, the industry has largely disappeared. Due to planning blight over many years the 'village' is very run down and the majority of the housing stock is 80 to 120 years old.

In 1910 the University of Birmingham was opened and this has grown considerably, particularly over the last 20 years, and now has in excess of 30,000 students. On the south side of the 'village' are the various Selly Oak colleges.

Church Beginnings

The church was planted in 1894 by members of the Wenman Street, Birmingham, 'Brethren' assembly (which disappeared in the city urban redevelopment of the 1960s) who regularly undertook open-air outreach work throughout rural Worcestershire. Originally, it was known as Tiverton Road Gospel Hall. It has always been independent and autonomous, its members and elders being mainly working class. Initially the believers met in one of the houses near the present chapel. They continued with open-air meetings and missions in the local area and also in the Birmingham Bull Ring. A purpose-built building was soon needed and this was erected on land donated by a local businessman. It was considerably extended in the 1960s, and some 10 years ago the houses on either side were purchased and are now let as flats for Christian students.

It is one of the few fellowships in the West Midlands to own its buildings, rather than renting them from an evangelical trust. As the original trustees retired or died, they were replaced by church members. The trust deeds were changed and now stipulate that trustees must be active members of the fellowship.

The original trustees were farseeing and 'open' in their views. The deeds stipulate that facilities for the exercise of *all* spiritual gifts must be provided and the supporting scriptures quoted leave no doubt as to what is meant. This proved to be an interesting point when spiritual gifts became an issue fifteen years ago. As the deeds seem to be derived from a standard model, it would be interesting to know if this was common to other assemblies of that era.

Maintaining The Status Quo

No formal records exist, and it seems that, until recent times, even proper accounts were not maintained. There are, however, members whose memory goes back to before 1910 and apparently membership remained consistently about 60–70 until the 1960s.

In the early 1960s, the status quo was only just about being maintained. This was probably due to the significant changes that were taking place in society at that time and the beginnings of the influence of the charismatic movement. The elders at that time were very godly and dedicated men, but perhaps lacked vision. The effects on the fellowship were largely seen in that individuals (1964) or small groups (1971) went off to set up or join other churches which offered a more open or pentecostal style of worship.

THE BEGINNINGS OF CHANGE

Around the time of Mission England (1983–4), the impetus for action was largely that of reaching out to those who were not Christians. It was realized that Tiverton Christian Fellowship (TCF) at that time would not be particularly attractive to the unchurched. The style of meeting was somewhat dated, and there was a rather insular attitude within the church. As a preparation for Mission England, changes were made. These involved changing the timing and style of the main outreach meeting to become a family service – in the hope that this would be a more attractive event than the traditional gospel meeting.

The impact of Mission England in terms of the number of new Christians coming and remaining with the church was very small. However, the process of change had begun, and various individuals were keen to see the church move on from its previous state.

One of the factors involved in on-going change was the exposure of individual church members to charismatic events outside the fellowship, while remaining within it. Significantly one of these people was part of the leadership team of the church. He showed maturity and patience in the way that changes were introduced. At first, it was by using some of the songs coming out of the charismatic movement, with the 'Harvest-time' songbook being used at times in worship, in addition to charismatic songs from the (comparatively non threatening!) Mission England songbook.

Various individuals in the church began attending extended events such as 'Spring Harvest', in addition to more local charismatic events. This outside influence came into the church like a breath of fresh air as a greater range of new songs was introduced, and a new freedom and vitality was experienced in the times of worship.

LEADING WORSHIP

The family service, which included a time of worship, came to be led in a way which went beyond the style of leading worship as a kind of chairman, announcing one song after another. Instead, it was conducted in a way which sought to be sensitive to the leading of the Holy Spirit, and to give a real lead to the congregation as it worshipped together. This style of leading worship was developed in the church by one of the leaders who, a few years previously, had been sceptical, if not antagonistic, towards the charismatic movement.

PARTICIPATION

The church sought to move away from the predictable 'hymn/ prayer/sermon and then all go home' format. Instead, the congregation was given an opportunity to respond at the end of a service, whether privately and individually, or through being given the opportunity to be prayed with.

During open worship times, 'pictures' which one person believed God had given him would sometimes be passed on to the church. In addition, although not prefaced by 'Thus says the Lord', there were occasions when a prophetic word was given, though in such terms that it might be seen by those who were not familiar with the charismatic movement as a general exhortation.

FELLOWSHIP

Within the church, people began to want – and enjoyed – greater times of fellowship with one another, as shown by the length of time they wanted to stay after a service had finished, talking and fellowshipping with one another.

PRAYER

There was a desire to make prayer times less formal, with worshipful and reflective prayers tending to replace 'shopping lists'. There was a greater readiness than previously to pray for people to be healed, and to expect God to work in miraculous ways. However, while individuals in the church use 'tongues' in their private prayer, this gift has not been used in a main church meeting where an interpretation would have been expected.

ROLE OF WOMEN

The role of women was another issue which needed to be addressed. The leadership was surprised at the number of people who had felt for many years that women should be permitted to pray, and take part audibly in services, but had graciously refrained from expressing their view in order to avoid causing offence.

INTRODUCING CHANGE

Thirty years ago, if asked, most members would probably have said that they held a cessationist view of the gifts of the Spirit, possibly because this had been taught since at least the early part of the century. Encouraging people to re-examine and change beliefs held for a lifetime was not an easy task, and changing some of the practices in the church had to be carried out carefully. There was a time during the transition when it seemed as if few people were really happy with the church. For some it was moving too slowly, and for others too quickly! However, moving gently, the elders were eventually able to issue a statement affirming that they believed that all the gifts of the Spirit were available today.

It is difficult to know how much the small resistance that was experienced was the result of a well thought out objection to the charismatic movement; how much of it was because of a vague fear of 'things charismatic'; and how much simply a resistance to changing the status quo. Perhaps, for some, the more direct and personal style in the services, especially when a response was invited, was quite threatening after years of being able to predict the course and outcome of a service. Whereas before, most calls for a response had been to non-Christians to become Christians, the challenge was now given to fairly comfortable Christians to examine their position and to change.

This new style of worship, with its different emphasis, did not please everyone. There was a time when this proved particularly difficult during extended open worship and, occasionally, it seemed as if the non-charismatic and the charismatic camps were each trying to stake out their territories, with one side appearing to keep the meeting as it had always been and the other side trying to adopt the new style. This proved difficult to control, given the nature of unstructured open worship.

Ministry to Students

With the local population comprising 70% students, one would expect church attendance to reflect this. Until 1970 one or, sometimes, two students, invariably from a 'Brethren' background would attend the church during their time at university. Today, the congregations comprise a large student element together with young professional couples who have moved near to the area or became involved with the fellowship while studying. The commitment of the young people is such that a significant number have joined as 'student members'. Over the past few years, on average, 5–10 baptisms have taken place each year.

The basic church membership is still about 60, but the large numbers attending the main service have created the need during term time to move this to the local community centre. The church sees a large turnover in students who stay for between 2 and 6 years, depending on the length of their courses. It has been described by one local minister as a 'Holy Spirit watering-hole' and the leadership recognizes the great responsibility and the unique ministry it has in pastoring and teaching so many gifted young people at the start of their career. The influence has already extended to every continent and all parts of the UK.

Bible Teaching

Much has been said of the changes made over the past two decades to the style of service, without which the church would not be in its present position and may even have ceased to exist. Alongside this, the Bible teaching ministry has also been developed to an unprecedented level and is well regarded by members and visitors.

The vast majority of the preaching and teaching is now conducted 'in house' as God has provided those with the necessary skills and gifting. This provides both continuity and variety and is probably the most significant factor in church life.

EVERY MEMBER MINISTRY

Emphasis is given to identifying the gifts of individuals and encouraging their use and development. No longer are the elders expected to be 'men of all trades' but are happy to delegate. Informal 'ministry' teams for such activities as teaching, visitation, prayer, evangelism, youth and student work, and worship are in operation.

CO-OPERATION WITH OTHER CHURCHES

A greater spirit of co-operation with other evangelical churches in the area than had ever been known before has ensued. This was initiated by the vicar of the nearby Anglican church, with fellowship also being enjoyed with the local Elim and Baptist churches. It takes the form of regular prayer lunches for church leaders, joint services and pulpit exchanges.

CONCLUSION

The elders are conscious that church life is a dynamic thing and, having seen the fellowship taken from the 1920s to the '90s in a period of ten years, wish to continue to move forward with the Lord. Regular reviews of progress and vision for the future are undertaken. Significantly, too, more jobs are being delegated with the intention that the elders should be able to devote more time to prayer and the spiritual direction of the church.

10

York Community Church

Don Palmer

*Raised in Belfast, N. Ireland, among 'Brethren' churches, Don
studied at Prairie Bible College, Alberta, Canada, where he gained a
Bachelor of Theology degree. Subsequently he has served as a
full-time worker at the Old Schoolhouse Christian Fellowship,
Edinburgh, and for the last six years at York Community Church.
Married to Kirstin, Don has two boys and is a keen supporter of
Leeds United. His book,* The Kingdom of God, *is currently
available through Evangelical Press.*

THE ROOTS – HOW WE WERE PLANTED

A popular board game was launched in 1997 called *Reminiscing*. It's
a really enjoyable memory-association game spanning the last four
decades. Its dubious subtitle is: 'A game for those old enough to
remember The Beatles. Suitable for age 12 and up'. Surely any
twelve-year-old would struggle to recall anything in the '80s, never
mind the '70s or '60! My memories of events in previous decades is
extremely limited, but 1993 will always live in my memory for in
November of that year York Community Church (YCC from here
on) was started.

Step back with me to the mid-'80s and a small struggling
'Brethren' church in the centre of York within the old historic city
walls. Faced with possible closure owing to failing numbers, a
group of the leaders prayed earnestly and decided to start taking
specific steps of faith based on a vision for the church. The three
stages they saw as necessary to translate this vision into reality, after
changing the name to St Andrew's Church, were: to discover ways
to make the services more relevant and to change their style; to
appoint a full-time worker; and eventually to plant another church.
I was invited in 1992 to join the church as full-time worker in

104

fulfilment of the second step in that plan. Few could have imagined that stage three would occur as soon as it did.

Near the end of my time in Edinburgh, God had graciouslv afforded me an opportunity to hear a team of three men from Chicago who had come to conduct a series of day seminars for select groups of church leaders. They were from Willow Creek Community Church. That day the Holy Spirit ignited a spark in my heart as I sat listening eagerly to the principles they humbly shared about how their church had grown over the past fifteen years. Here was no triumphalist American sensationalism, but a group of meek men sharing their passion for reaching lost people and creating a 'church for the unchurched' where God had placed them. If God ignited the spark in Edinburgh that Monday morning, he truly lit the fire that summer in Birmingham where I attended the first major Willow Creek conference to be held in the UK. Since then, Willow Creek's vision for evangelism and its principles for re-thinking the whole way we 'do church' have taken hold of many church leaders in our nation. I would say that not since Mission England in the early '80s with Billy Graham has there been a greater evangelistic impact on the church in this country. Even Alpha is seeker-sensitive evangelism.

Returning to York I shared this vision first with my fellow elders and then with other key individuals in the church. It was warmly received and we prayerfully considered how to implement some of these principles in our context. As we began to do so, it soon became evident that St. Andrew's was not the place where we could do it. A number of other changes were taking place within that fellowship, but this is not the time or place to be specific. Suffice it to say that during the summer and autumn of 1993 we seriously considered planting a new church altogether, in a community somewhere in York.

As we surveyed the city, seeking to ascertain where there was a lack of any real evangelical work and which areas seemed to have the greatest need and present the greatest challenge, our minds were drawn to a large working-class housing estate on the east side of the city. Significantly, many of us lived in that general area. We started by holding family services in a local secondary school on a couple of occasions. These were well-attended and quite successful. Soon after, we became aware of the availability of the local Tang Hall Community Centre, and after negotiations booked the centre with the intention of holding services and gradually planting a new church. At the time, some judged the move premature, but on reflection we can see it was 'just at the right time' (Gal 4:4) in God's agenda. Another example of God's gracious timing was the fact that we were able to have our annual church away weekend that November, as we were embarking on this new initiative. We used that opportunity to lay clearly before all who were joining us what was going to be involved in this new work and to pray through several issues. On 7 November our journey of faith was to commence.

I can still recall that first Sunday morning as about fifty of us gathered, with a box of *Mission Praise* hymn books and a borrowed keyboard in a cold building – they obviously weren't used to a group using the place on a Sunday – with the local Karate club posters surrounding us on the walls, to worship the Lord. Since then we have grown and become a thriving community holding three Sunday services, but we still maintain our practice of commencing Sunday (and, to an extent, the week's activities) by worshipping God and praising him for what he has done in and through us by his grace, mercy and power.

I also recall our first business meeting when probably the most difficult decision to make was what we should call ourselves. The decisive factor was what the local people could relate to. The chosen name summarizes what it is all about. We are first of all a church, namely a group of people who believe in and follow Jesus Christ; second we are based in York and wish to be identified with all other Christian churches in that city who are seeking to be witnesses of Jesus Christ; and third we believe God has called us to be a Christian presence in the community of Tang Hall and to see the kingdom of God grow in that area.

Before moving on to share how and why we grew, I want to mention one other important point. In July 1993 I had the privilege of attending the Partnership consultation in Warwick with another elder, Alex McIlhinney. During the consultation we both sensed God touch us and reaffirm the rightness of the step of faith we were about to take. At Warwick, a small group of us from Yorkshire met to pray through how we could move forward by sharing some of the challenges and principles we were learning at the consultation. Subsequently we started holding day conferences and elders' retreats specifically for the Yorkshire region. To date we have held five conferences with keynote speakers, and two elders' days. Early in 1999 our Yorkshire conference took the form of a joint conference with another local group who are trying to follow the Willow Creek principles in their services and evangelism. In some ways we feel we have come full circle.

Partnership has provided us with invaluable stimulus and support, and has served as an 'umbrella' under which we have been able to gather with leaders of churches similar to our own during the past six years. (If you are reading this and your church is still seeking to function independently, my advice would be to consult Partnership immediately and avail yourselves of the services they are offering to independent churches in the UK and across the world.)

THE FRUIT – HOW WE GREW

I still recall one of the leaders from Willow Creek sharing a poignant thought at that original conference I attended in Edinburgh. He said that we all realise that scripture teaches there is a 'great gulf' (Luke 16:26) between humanity and God. Nothing we can do can bridge that gap – only the sacrifice of Christ is sufficient. However, not many people in our society have any real understanding of that fact. So how will they know? The trouble is that there exists a 'not-so-great-gulf' between these same people and the church! We certainly can't bridge the first gap, but we should be concerned about building bridges between these people and us, so that the second gap is filled!

Sadly, it is often the case that when people start crossing the bridge we have built and come into our churches. what they see, hear and experience drives them straight back across the bridge as fast as they can go, never to be seen again! A survey done by Peter Brierley not so long ago on church-going and beliefs in Britain revealed the remarkable fact that the proportion of people who said they believed in God (approx. 80% of those surveyed) was almost identical with the percentage of those who said they never went to church. This suggests that many in our society still have some kind of belief in God, but they are certainly not going to church to find him.

Our approach can be summarised by two quotations. The first of these, taken from our *Guide to belonging to YCC* booklet is:

We aim to share the good news of God's love and forgiveness through Jesus Christ with all whom we contact. To this end we organize a family service each Sunday at 11.15am where the focus is to challenge people to enter a relationship with God and to live His way. We also arrange a number of special social events to which we can invite friends to hear the Christian faith, again shared in a relevant way. We encourage all who join us to be witnesses and share their faith as opportunity arises. We too recognize the importance of encouraging people to grow in their faith and become disciples (that is, mature followers of Jesus Christ).

The other is our *Mission Statement*, which reads:

We aim, through a process of discipleship, to bring those not yet Christians into a relationship with God and teach them how to live his way; so extending his kingdom in our community.

These two statements summarise not only what we wish to achieve at YCC but also how we aim to achieve it. Our purpose is to reach unchurched people and help them mature as Christians within the body of Christ. The means we use to make these aims become reality are just as important. I shared at that initial church weekend in the Yorkshire Dales in November 1993 the following essential steps about church growth:

- Have a vision, and share it.

- Establish your aims and goals.

- Develop a strategy to achieve your goals and support your aims.

- Work out your plan (and stay focused).

- Assess your results regularly.

The steps we have chosen to adopt to achieve our goals are first of all to create an environment on Sunday mornings at 11:15 where unchurched people can feel comfortable, hear and see a relevant message for their lives, and come to understand that they matter to God (who has done all that is necessary for them to come to know him and live his way). Willow Creek call this their 'seeker-service'. We don't use that terminology, but the aim is the same.

We determined to face up to this challenge by providing an occasion when people could come to a church service whose content is challenging and faithful to scripture, but whose form they can relate to. A small task group in YCC is responsible to think creatively about our 11:15 service and use whatever means are necessary to ensure that it communicates relevantly with those who attend. We use drama, audience participation, performed music, video-projected images and videos, overhead transparencies, interviews, puppetry, dramatised readings and anything else appropriate to prepare those present to hear God's word for that day. Unlike Willow Creek, we still use worship and regularly sing both hymns and modern worship songs. That service is a vital ingredient in what we do as a church. It is now packed out most Sundays, to the point where we must seriously consider whether to put on another service, move to a larger building or plant another church!

A few words of warning. Whatever you do, do it well. Be organised, and be prepared to spend time planning and practising. It will call for a lot of hard work, and it will cost time and money, Choose speakers carefully, for they must be able to communicate in jargon-free language. Spurgeon once said that, as Christians, we should hold our Bible in one hand and a newspaper in the other! In other words, the challenge is to be faithful to the word, but relevant to the world.

We are very conscious that one service a week, no matter how powerful, will not change people's lives long-term. Therefore we must have in place an effective system of discipleship. This word has become vital to us over the past five years. It is something that most of us believe in and have probably heard about, but are we practising it within our churches? Do we structure ourselves for real one-to-one discipleship? Before going to the Cross, Jesus said in his upper-room prayer, 'I have ... completed the work you gave me to do.' (John 17:4) What work? He had not yet died or risen! I believe he is speaking here about the work of discipleship. In fact he immediately proceeds to pray for these men who had spent just over three years with him. If any decision or commitment is going to bear lasting fruit, a process of discipleship must take place in that individual's life. The Alpha course has taught us this as it takes 'seekers' through basic Christian beliefs over a period of several weeks. So we seek to link individuals up as soon as possible (even prior to conversion if necessary) with someone who will meet with them, share with them, be available to them and lead them through a basic course in discipleship. Many good courses are available, and if you cannot find one that suits you, you can always write your own.

We also believe in the importance of prayer as a basis for hearing God and seeking his blessing and anointing on all our activities. Apart from prayer in our services, individually, and in house groups and other small groups, we book a hall the first Saturday of each month and meet for one hour to pray specifically about the needs of the community, and the work of our church and other local churches. We have also engaged in prayer walks from time to time.

Something else which we have learned by experience is the need to be prepared to break with our inherited practices and start mixing with unchurched people. This may mean joining a local club or society; having someone round for a coffee; doing their shopping; looking after their children; helping them mend something broken. It may even mean going with them to a pub for a social drink – something we have found quite successful on a number of occasions. Pub quizzes are very popular in our area. So from time to time we run one with refreshments laid on in a function room of a local pub. People can order their own drinks. At the end of the evening we have had a selection of interesting, relevant local speakers who have shared an aspect of their faith. These events are always well-attended. We have also developed ongoing links with local schools which regularly invite us to take assemblies and give lessons, and with several nursing homes where we go every week to take services.

We produce a church community newsletter called *Impact* which is distributed to several thousand homes about three times a year. On occasion we have also surveyed several streets with a basic questionnaire or to offer the 'Jesus' video for use in homes. Not many have taken us up on this offer, but we have met some interesting and unusual people whom we would not have met otherwise. Since our last visits, three new people attend our church and we are convinced they have come to know the Lord. Door-to-door work, as it is traditionally called, has received a lot of bad press in recent years and still proves very daunting for certain Christians. However, we have found that it makes the task easier and more effective if one or two streets are targeted, and something specific is offered. Currently, we are considering another survey in co-operation with other local churches to assess people's felt needs and try to discover ways of meeting those needs.

As we have studied the example of the early church (Acts 2:42ff, 4:32ff) we could hardly fail to notice their social compassion and personal involvement. So we have sought ways to get involved with people in our local community. We have done this directly with families and individuals in need. We have also discovered a local family centre which assists some of those in most extreme poverty in our community. At certain times of the year we take them food, clothes and toy packages for distribution. Again, the challenge is to be seen in the local community as being relevant. People will listen to our words when they see our works.

Apart from local working-class people, the other main grouping of people to whom God has clearly led us is students. We are within ten minutes' walk of the campus of York University. We have seen a number of students come to faith, and many baptisms; quite a few enlist in discipleship courses; and several each year get involved in our various church ministries (especially with local kids and teenagers). We have been greatly blessed by their enthusiasm and commitment to the Lord. During each of the last three years we have taken on a student for a year's placement with us as a youth worker. This has worked well for us and has given the individual a year of experience, working with a local church in schools and the community. Incidentally, grants are available to assist churches in doing this.

CONCLUSION

As I bring to an end this whistle-stop tour of the brief history of YCC I am conscious that there is much more that I could say. We have experienced the heartache of seeing individuals fall away; encountered virtually every social evil the human mind can imagine; and known times of stress, illness and trial within the families of our church. We have made a number of mistakes, which is inevitable when we change course and embark on the task of planting a church. But, thanks be to God, we have stayed focused to our vision and mission and have preserved a real unity and love among the church family. We have also learned much through these experiences over the past five years – lessons which we might not have been able to learn through a textbook.

Harold Rowdon said to us about four years ago at a local Partnership conference, 'I believe people are looking to belong before they are looking to believe', and we can testify to the truth of that statement. Many of the individuals we encounter have been rejected by parents, friends, partners and even society. In our Father God they find one who accepts them just like the prodigal into his family. As communities of the King we need to model that acceptance and show them we care. Only then, when they cross the bridges we erect, will they see the greater bridge of the Cross of Christ (1Tim 2:5) and move over it by the grace of God.

Partnership Publications

*Partnership publications may be obtained from Paternoster Press,
PO Box 300, Carlisle, Cumbria, CA3 0QS (Tel: 01228 512 512;
Fax: 01228-514949; Web:http://paternoster-publishing.com)*

A full listing of Partnership Publications appears below:

Editor: Peter Brierley

The Christian Brethren as the Nineties Began

The results of a 1988 survey of independent congregations in the British
Isles set alongside the relevant statistics of the 1989 English church
census present not only useful information on the current state of the
Brethren Movement, but also indications as to future developments.

0-900128-09-7 / pb / iv+112pp / 229 × 145 mm / £6.99

Neil Dickson

Modern Prophetesses

Women Preachers in the Nineteenth-Century Scottish Brethren
(Partnership Booklets)

0-900128-14-3 / pb / 28pp / 210 × 145 mm / £1.50

Kevin G. Dyer

Must Brethren Churches Die?

After an introductory chapter by John Allan, the author analyses four
factors which must characterize healthy churches—unity, leadership,
change and vision—and asks the question: What must be done to
rekindle the flame which is in danger of going out?

0-900128-08-9 / pb / 79pp / 210 × 145 mm / £4.99

Jonathan Lamb

Making Progress in Church Life
How to Handle Change Positively

The author writes in his Introduction, 'Wise Christian leadership seems to me to be a marriage of the pastoral and the strategic. By this I mean it is vitally important to set biblical priorities and direction for our churches, but this is to be done in the context of a care for each member of the congregation. The pastoral metaphor of the shepherd, so familiar to the biblical writers, contains elements of both leadership and care which are specially needed in handling change positively'.

0-900128-17-8 / stitched / 48pp / 210 × 148 mm / £3.50

Cedric Longville

Go Tell My Brothers—
Christian Women and Church Worship

It is commonly held that the apostle Paul ruled against women speaking publicly in church worship. The author here sizes up the traditional arguments for this position against the biblical material pertinent to the question, starting with the accounts of the first witnesses of the risen Christ. His conclusion, a challenge to rethink widely-held views, seeks to do justice to Christ's status as sole head of his worshipping people. Cedric Longville is a Christian lawyer living in Cardiff.

0-900128-13-5 / pb / xiv + 142pp / 229 × 145 mm / £7.99

Henry Ratter

Buried Talents
Or, *God Given Gifts for Building His Church*

The author, a chemical engineer working with ICI, has been involved in numerous roles, including the leadership of business teams and human resource development. In this brief book he brings his experience to bear on the problem of developing individual talent in the local church. Valuable Appendixes include *Job Profiles*, *Analysing Your Gift*, *Training Materials* and *Work Analysis*. A highly practical, biblically based little manual.

0-900128-18-6 / stitched / 71pp / 210 × 148 mm / £4.99

Olive Rogers, Sally Hogg et al

Does God Expect Less of Women?

Until recently the church certainly did 'expect less' of women than it did of men. There is a good deal of evidence that some Christians still do. This series of Bible studies goes beyond details of practice to investigate biblical principles.

0-900128-15-1 / pb / 32pp / 210 × 148mm / £2.99

D D Ronco

Risorgimento and the Free Italian Churches, now Churches of the Brethren

A fascinating historical study from an expert in the field. *(Available from: Dr D D Ronco, 1 Hendyrpeg, Penmyndd Road, Menai Bridge, Gwynedd LL59 5RU).*

Editor: Harold H. Rowdon

The Brethren Contribution to the Worldwide Mission of the Church

This collection of papers is a record of the International Brethren Conference on Missions held at the Anglo-Chinese School in Singapore. Issues covered are biblical and theological, historical, ideological, and practical.

0-900128-12-7 / pb / 127pp / 229 × 145mm / £5.99

Editor: Harold H. Rowdon

Churches in Partnership for Strengthening and Growth

A follow-up to the Nantwich Consultation, these are the edited papers of a consultation held at the University of Warwick. Themes covered include inter-church co-operation, the training of leaders, and openness to other traditions.

0-900128-11-9 / pb / 80pp / 229 × 145mm / £4.99

Editor: Harold H. Rowdon

Declare His Glory
Congregational Worship Today

Fifteen years ago, *Partnership* recognised the urgent need for biblical reflection and practical advice on the subject of worship, and published the first edition of *Declare His Glory*.

This new edition is a major development of the original, with a new Introduction by Jonathan Lamb, a completely new chapter on worship and the Lord's Supper, and revised and much-expanded material on the practice of worship today. John Baigent's thorough biblical foundation for worship remains, as does John Allan's brilliant treatment of music, movement and silence in worship, and Peter Cousins' reflections on worship and life.

0-900128-20-8 / pb / 144pp / 216 × 135 mm / £8.99

Editor: Harold H. Rowdon

Don't Muzzle the Ox
Full-time Ministry in Local Churches

This book provides valuable guidance for churches planning to appoint full-time workers. Biblical principles are clearly spelled out, whilst matters relating to selection and appointment are dealt with in detail.

The book moves on to examine working relationships with other local church leaders, the full-time worker's spirituality and effective use of time.

Though written primarily for churches with a Brethren background, *Don't Muzzle the Ox* contains material, much of it not readily available elsewhere, useful for any church seeking full-time help.

0-9001280-19-4 / pb / 108pp / 229 × 145 mm / £4.99

Editor: Harold H. Rowdon

The Strengthening, Growth and Planting of Local Churches

Papers on key issues facing independent congregations, such as leadership, youth work, women in the church, church-planting models, and race, class and social character.

0-900128-10-0 / pb / 141pp / 210 × 145mm / £6.99

Neil Summerton

Local Churches for a New Century
A Strategic Challenge

After describing briefly the present situation in Brethren churches and its origins, the author present readers with a series of strategic pointers for the next century, challenging them with fresh insights on subjects as diverse as spirituality, cultural relevance, worship, pastoral care, the role of women and effective communication.

0-900128-16-X / stitched / 23pp / 216 × 148 mm / £2.50

Neil Summerton

A Noble Task
Eldership and Ministry in the Local Church (Revised Edition)

'I would urge everyone involved with local church leadership and developments in local ministry to read A Noble Task—*for its inspiration, practical common sense, and balanced biblical analysis of important ministry issues.'*— Churchman

0-85364-515-9 / pb / 213pp / 216 × 135mm / £9.99

Christian Brethren Review Backlist

41. *Scottish Brethren 1838–1916 and other papers.* (£4.00)

40. *Into all the world. Papers on world mission today: understanding it, practising it, teaching it.* (£4.50)

39. *Declare His glory: A fresh look at our congregational worship.* (First edition) (£4.00)

38. *Handling differences: How to disagree without disintegrating.* (£2.00)

37. *Servants of God: Papers on the use of full-time workers in Brethren churches.* (First edition, 1986) (£3.50)

36. *World Mission Today: The challenge of mission today, its biblical basis, training, accountability.* (£3.50)

35. *The Caring Church: Papers on counselling and pastoral care.* (£3.50)

31–32. *The Bible in the Eighties.* (£3.50)

29. *Neo-Pentecostalism/Urban Evangelism.* (£1.50)

28. *The Biblical doctrine of man/John Synge and the early Brethren.* (£1.00)

27. *Sex Ethics.* (£1.50)

Brethren Archivists and Historians
Network Review

Membership of the Brethren Archivists and Historians Network is open for an annual subscription of £UK10 to residents of the British Isles and £16 (at the particular rate of exchange prevailing at any time) for those located elsewhere. Applications and subscriptions should be sent to Neil Dickson, 6 Belleisle Place, Kilmarnock, Ayrshire KA1 4UD, UK.

Occasional papers (new series)

Peter Brierley, *Growing churches at the July 1993 Warwick Consultation.* (£1.00, p & p inc.) *Available from the Executive Chairman of Partnership, Dr Neil Summerton, 52 Hornsey Lane London N6 5LU.*

Publications Archive Listing

A hand list of all Christian Brethren Research Fellowship and Partnership publications since 1963 is available from the Executive Chairman of Partnership, Dr Neil Summerton, 52 Hornsey Lane, London N6 5LU—who will also be pleased to receive membership subscriptions (£20 per annum for individuals; and 80p per annum per member for corporate subscription by local churches (subject to a minimum payment of £30 for churches of 38 members/regular attenders or less, and a maximum of £90 for churches with more than 112 members/regular attenders)).

Library Deposits

CBRF and Partnership publications are deposited with the British Library, the National Library of Wales and the National Library of Scotland, and can also be seen at the Christian Brethren Archive of the John Rylands University Library, University of Manchester, Oxford Road, Manchester M13 9PP (contact David Brady). Dr Brady is happy to be contacted about access to items which are out of print, and also about access to the manuscript collections included in the Archive.

Tapes

Tapes of addresses given at CBRF and Partnership national seminars and consultations are available from D J Scott, 40 Bakewell Road, Hazel Grove, Stockport, SK7 6JU (price £1.50 per item, plus £0.50p per order postage and packing). A list of tapes is available from him or from the Executive Secretary.

Back Copy Availability

Subject to availability, back copies of Partnership Newsletters (New Series) and *Partnership Perspectives* (the magazine which has replaced the new series of newsletters) can be obtained from the Executive Secretary, price £1.25 per item (+ £0.25p postage and packing).